our Stories remember

American Indian History, Culture,
and Values through Storytelling

D1115718

JOSEPH BRUCHAC

Earlier versions of "Indians and Art" and "Timeline: Development of Native Art in North America" first appeared in *Creative Classroom*. Earlier versions of "Between the Worlds," "The Place of the Art," and "Spirit: Life and Death" first appeared in *Parabola*.

Library of Congress Cataloging-in-Publication Data

Bruchac, Joseph, 1942–
  Our stories remember : American Indian history, culture, and values
through storytelling / Joseph Bruchac.
      p. cm.
Includes bibliographical references.
  ISBN 1-55591-129-3 (pbk. : alk. paper)
  1. Indians of North America—History. 2. Indians of North
America—Folklore. 3. Indians of North America—Social life and customs. I. Title.
E77.B873 2003
973.04'97—dc21   2002151236

Printed in the United States of America
0 9 8 7 6 5 4 3 2 1

Editorial: Ellen Wheat, Linda Gunnarson
Cover and interior design: Elizabeth Watson
Interior formatting: Anne Clark
Map: Marge Mueller, Gray Mouse Graphics
Cover photographs: *foreground*—gull feather in grasses, twilight, Cape Krusenstern National
  Monument, Alaska, copyright © 1999 Pat O'Hara; *background*—close up of photograph of
  Antoine Janis in top hat with Oglala Sioux Indians, 1877, photographer unknown, courtesy
  of Fort Collins Public Library, Fort Collins, Colorado.

Fulcrum Publishing
16100 Table Mountain Parkway, Suite 300
Golden, Colorado 80403
(800) 992-2908 • (303) 277-1623
www.fulcrum-books.com

contents

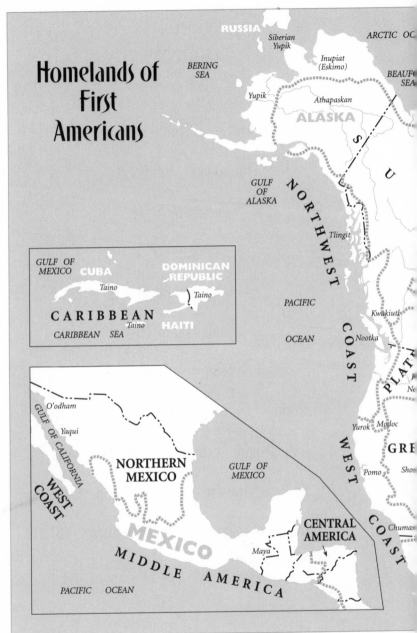

Homelands of First Americans

RUSSIA

Siberian Yupik

ARCTIC OC.

Inupiat (Eskimo)

BERING SEA

BEAUFO SEA

Yupik

Athapaskan

ALASKA

S

U

GULF OF ALASKA

NORTHWEST

Tlingit

PACIFIC

Kwakiutl

GULF OF MEXICO

CUBA

DOMINICAN REPUBLIC

Taino

OCEAN

Nootka

COAST

Taino

CARIBBEAN

PLAT

Taino

Ne

CARIBBEAN SEA

HAITI

Yurok

Modoc

WEST

GRE

O'odham

Pomo

Shos

GULF OF CALIFORNIA

Yaqui

NORTHERN MEXICO

GULF OF MEXICO

COAST

WEST COAST

CENTRAL AMERICA

Chumas

MEXICO

Maya

PACIFIC OCEAN

MIDDLE AMERICA

This map does not show all of the more than 500 tribal nations of North America, but only those mentioned in the text, plus a few representative others. Due to space constraints, the locations of some tribes are approximate.

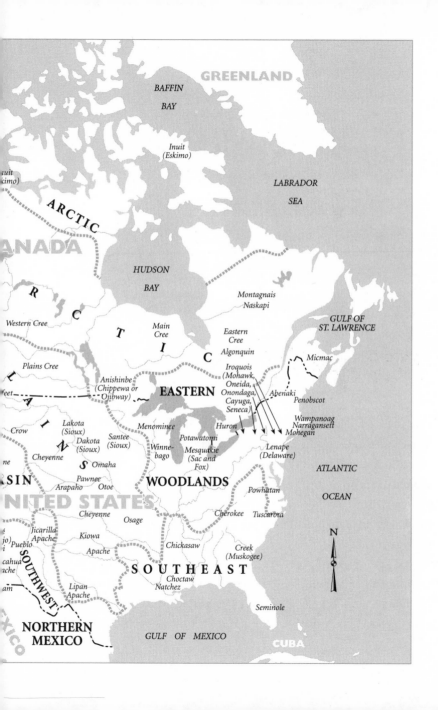

GREENLAND

BAFFIN
BAY

Inuit
(Eskimo)

LABRADOR
SEA

ARCTIC

Inuit
(Eskimo)

CANADA

HUDSON
BAY

Montagnais
Naskapi

GULF OF
ST. LAWRENCE

Western Cree

Main
Cree

Eastern
Cree

Micmac

Plains Cree

Anishinbe
(Chippewa or
Ojibway)

EASTERN

Iroquois
(Mohawk,
Oneida,
Onondaga,
Cayuga,
Seneca)

Abenaki

Penobscot

Wampanoag
Narragansett
Mohegan

Lakota
(Sioux)

Menominee

Huron

Crow

Dakota
(Sioux)

Santee
(Sioux)

Winne-
bago

Potawatomi

Lenape
(Delaware)

ATLANTIC

Cheyenne

Omaha

Mesquakie
(Sac and
Fox)

OCEAN

Pawnee

Otoe

WOODLANDS

Powhatan

BASIN

Arapaho

UNITED STATES

Cheyenne

Osage

Cherokee

Tuscarora

Jicarilla
Apache

Kiowa

Navajo
Pueblo

Apache

Chickasaw

Creek
(Muskogee)

N

Chiricahua
Apache

SOUTHWEST

SOUTHEAST

Choctaw

Lipan
Apache

Natchez

Seminole

NORTHERN
MEXICO

GULF OF MEXICO

CUBA

MEXICO

introduction: connections

Humans make but little.
They think they know much.

All things declare
Mu'ndu had made them.

I cannot make myself,
they declare.
Humans cannot make one tree.

—*Fidelia Fielding/Flying Bird (Mohegan), 1925*

"I have a friend." Those are words that take on a different meaning in American Indian culture. In the old Indian sense of the word, friend (*Nidoba,* or "my friend," as we say in Abenaki) implies a deep and sacred relationship of trusting, sharing, and mutual support. A friend is a person you tell your true name. Lance Henson, a Cheyenne writer whose poems are as deeply loved in Europe as in the United States, is a friend of mine like that. Although there are times when Lance is, quite frankly, a pain in the ass, I am pretty sure there have been times (like when I'm being the Anti-cigarette Squad) he's found me just as tiresome. But if I had to go into battle, I'd want a friend like Lance by my side. I hope he feels the same.

I mention Lance to begin with because there's a story I'd like you to read right at the start of this book, a story that has Lance and me in it, but a story that is meant for you.

introduction: connections

It was a hot Oklahoma day and we were in Lance's Jeep Renegade, on our way to do a writing workshop for Indian inmates at MacAllister Prison. Seemingly out of nowhere (though I know there had to be a context for it), Lance turned to me and asked, "Joe, are you carrying around any guilt about anything?"

I thought about it for a minute, maybe longer. Silence is a pretty good thing to seek help from when you get asked a tough question like that. Finally I had my answer. "No," I said. "I'm not."

Lance smiled at that. "Brother, that's good," he said. "One of my elders asked me once what you should do with a cup of water that is not good to drink." He held his hand as if holding that cup and then tipped it over, pouring it out. "That's the Cheyenne Way."

Don't keep carrying something that is of no use to anyone.

And what does that have to do with the pages that follow? Simply this: that an awful lot of Americans feel guilt about what their ancestors did to American Indians. That guilt either makes them feel sad or it makes them angry and ready to deny it. It makes them turn away from the truth because they find it too painful or don't want to accept it. Guilt works that way. It clouds your vision with sorrow or twists your thoughts with defensive anger.

Yes, tough things have happened to American Indian people. Yes, maybe some of your ancestors had something to do with it. But, like that Cheyenne teaching tells us, there comes a time to get rid of that which cannot help us and refill our cups with life. Listen, be concerned, take some positive action of your own to make things better—even if it involves only being more mindful of what you do and say, more respectful of other beings—but don't feel guilty. If anything you read in the following pages makes you feel guilty, then we've both failed, writer and reader alike.

Pour out your cup. Hold it out empty. Fill it with stories.

our stories remember

Anyone who writes a book about the entirety of American Indian experience needs to make some qualifying statements right at the start. These are mine.

First, I fully realize that I do not know enough, have not lived long enough, and never will experience enough in my brief lifetime to do full justice to any discussion of our many nations, our many stories. Because of that, you will find me relying on the words and writings of others in the pages that follow. Though I lean in this way on many shoulders, I am still aware of how inadequate my efforts may appear.

Second, I cannot stress enough the fact that there is really no such thing as *The* American Indian or *The* Native American. Seeing all Indians as being alike is as foolish as not being able to see them at all. (Non-Indian Americans are deeply prone to both failures of vision.) The American Indian world is more complex than most people realize. I think of the story told to me two years ago by a teacher I know in Arizona. (She asked me to not mention her name or the school where she taught.) A teenage Navajo student was having some "adjustment problems." The school administrators thought they had the perfect, sensitive, culturally appropriate solution: They had just hired an American Indian counselor from a nearby tribe. But when they tried to send the boy to him for guidance, to their surprise, both the boy and the counselor were uncomfortable about this "politically correct" solution. Why? Because the boy was Navajo and the counselor was Ute. It was the Utes who raided the Navajos for many generations, who were the Indian scouts for the U.S. Army in the 1860s when the Navajos were sent on the terrible Long Walk to a concentration camp in New Mexico, and who remain disliked and distrusted by many Navajos. Both the Navajo boy and the Ute counselor agreed that a white counselor was better suited to the job.

Native America is made up of many cultures, hundreds of them. There is not just one history of the American Indian but countless histories. Moreover, those histories are not static, but growing and changing, adding new layers of growth each year just as living trees do. There are so many stories, as many as the leaves on those trees. And all of them remain rooted in this soil, this earth that has never been given up by the people. I do not think that I am exaggerating about the depth of Native American story traditions. The Native tales that have been recorded on paper by Europeans number in the thousands, a process that began more than five centuries ago. And storytelling among the more than three hundred living Indian nations of the United States has not ended. New stories and new storytellers are born every day.

Third, although our diversity remains, there is more intertribalism among the Native nations of this continent today than at any other time in our histories. That intertribalism, in fact, is largely responsible for making a book such as this possible. It is impossible for me to name and fully credit every American Indian elder, teacher, and friend who has shared his or her knowledge with me in an intertribal spirit over the past five decades. You'll find mention of many in these pages, but you should know that there are many, many more and that it is only the fault of my weak memory if I fail to do justice to their generosity of spirit.

What has driven that increased contemporary intertribalism? I see it as a result of a number of processes, some of which have always been here on this continent and some of which are a direct and crucial result of European colonization:

Past connections. Ancient links between American Indian nations were made through trade and travel, resulting in the dissemination of stories and important food crops such as the maize that was developed first in the Valley of Mexico, and through the development of a number of quite similar sign languages, which existed in the Northeast, the Southeast, the Great Plains, the Great Lakes, and the Northwest. Connections were also formed, at times involuntarily, when members of one tribal nation were taken as captives and then adopted into a new tribe. Full adoption was a common practice, one that was often wholeheartedly accepted by the adopted individuals, especially if they were taken when they were young.

our stories remember

(This practice of captive adoption would later be applied to Europeans, producing a number of "white Indians" who bonded so thoroughly with their new families that they refused to return to white culture and even aided their adoptive peoples in war against the whites. Those well-known white Indians include Samuel Gill, a ten-year-old boy captured in Massachusetts by the Abenakis in 1697, and a little girl known only as "Miss James," who was taken prisoner in Maine about the same time. Both children were adopted and raised in the Abenaki Way. The two married and one of their sons, Joseph-Louis Gill, rose to a position of leadership, becoming famous as the "White Chief of the St. Francis," an important figure in peace and war during the last half of the eighteenth century. Perhaps the best-known white captive who lived out her life among her adopted people was Mary Jemison, the "White Lady of the Senecas." Taken by the Shawnees in 1758 at the age of sixteen and then adopted by the Senecas, she was given the name "Two Falling Voices." She fully accepted Indian life, married happily, became an influential voice among the matriarchal Iroquois, and had many children. The remarkable tale of her long life was published in 1824 by Dr. James Everett Seaver after interviewing Mary Jemison in 1823. *A Narrative of the Life of Mrs. Mary Jemison* was a bestseller and remains in print to this day. Ironically, despite the fact that she was given a Seneca name, her Indian descendants opted to use her last name. Today there are thousands of her descendants among the Iroquois and more than half a dozen variant forms of her name, including Jemison, Jamieson, and Jimmerson, among the Senecas.)

Shared world views. The predominant world view shared by the majority of American Indian nations is that of the circularity of existence. It is a universe in which, as Black Elk put it, "the Power of the world always works in a circle and everything tries to be round." The cycle of the seasons, the circling of sun and moon, even the round shapes of the nests of birds are evidence of this. Just as every point on a circle is equal to every other point, no place being closer to the center than any other, all created things are regarded as being of equal importance. All things—not only humans and animals and plants, but even the winds, the waters, fire, and the stones—are living and sentient. Further, just as the strands of a spider web are so interconnected that touching one makes all the others tremble, in that circular universe everything is connected to everything else.

Human beings are a natural part of this living and aware world, and vice versa. The importance of the family, an extended family, the realization that cooperation is the best way to live as human beings, and the recognition that no individual is more important than his or her people, are also universal truths among American Indian tribal nations. Spiritual growth, rather than materialism, is stressed. The deep connection of each Indian nation to its own land is part of this spiritual and non-materialistic view. Remaining with their sacred land and protecting it became a central concern for one Indian nation after another during the centuries of resistance (which have not yet ended).

Common or deeply similar colonial and post-colonial histories. Among American Indian nations, when Europeans arrived and began settling on the land, a pattern emerged that repeated itself again and again across the continent:
- The first whites were welcomed.
- That welcome was repaid by aggression and ingratitude.
- The Indian people were forced into resistance.
- Superior white weaponry and European diseases overcame Native resistance.
- The Indian nation was decimated and forced into slavery or driven off its land by one means or another. (This process of removal did not always end with one dislocation, but sometimes happened several times—as with the Mahicans, who left the Hudson Valley for Stockbridge, Massachusetts, then had to seek shelter among the Oneidas of New York, and finally, after

the American Revolution, had to move to Wisconsin to the contemporary Stockbridge Munsee Reservation.)

- A reservation was established, often on the poorest soil and in the most inaccessible locations.
- Indian children were taken from their families and placed in boarding schools or adopted by whites.
- The survival of Indian languages and traditions became threatened.

Indian boarding schools. It is hard to exaggerate how important, how traumatic, and how significant the Indian boarding school experiment was. Instituted as a federal program when the last Indian wars of the nineteenth century were drawing to a close, the purpose of these schools was to civilize the Indians by a new battle plan. (Military terms are appropriate here.) The continued resistance of Indian leaders, and Indian adults in general, to government attempts to force them into new ways of life convinced a number of prominent whites that a new tactic was needed. The older generation, they argued, was hopeless. Forget them, let them die off. The attack would be on the young. By sending Indian children to boarding schools, often hundreds of miles away from their homes, by separating them from the insidious influence of their cultures—their native dress, their languages, their parents and grandparents—they would be more easily molded into new civilized people, lesser images of the nineteenth-century white men and women who saw themselves as the paragons of all that was good and virtuous, the perfection of humanity.

However, the boarding schools did more than foster among its unwilling attendees the white definition of being civilized. The shared suffering of generations of Indian students forced to attend schools with Indians from dozens of different tribes from all around the continent fostered a better understanding of shared values and led to a new sense of intertribalism. Further, that first small step into white-style education began the process of understanding and making use of the American democratic system, which would see American Indian lawyers winning land rights cases and defending traditional cultures in the last third of the twentieth century. It could be said that the American Indian political organizations of the twentieth century—from the American Indian Movement (AIM) to the National Congress of American Indians and the Native American Rights Fund—were born in the boarding schools.

Writing. Connections among the different tribal nations of North America, or at least a wider awareness of how other Indians live, have also been fed by the written word. If you go into Indian homes today, you will often see at least one or two overflowing bookcases. In those bookcases are not only books written by non-natives about their people (I remember how my friend Dewasentah, an Onondaga Clan Mother, had not only just about every book written by white scholars about her people, but also a very clear, incisive, and well-stated opinion about each of them. Academic ears must have been burning during some of our conversations!), but also books written by American Indian authors from their own tribe and others—perhaps a book of free verse by the Pueblo poet Simon Ortiz, who said in one of his poems, "Indians are everywhere." From the sixteenth century (with the publication in Spanish of two major titles by Garcilaso de la Vega, the son of a Spaniard and an Inca noblewoman) to the present, American Indians have been writing about their histories, their stories, their lives.

The modern wave of Indian book publication (and I am not speaking of "as told to" books, but books fully authored by Native people) began rolling in at the end of the nineteenth century with Zitkala-sa/Gertrude Bonnin (Lakota), Francis LaFlesche (Omaha), and Charles Eastman/Ohiyesa (Dakota); and continued in the 1920s and 1930s with Luther Standing Bear (Lakota), who wrote quite eloquently of his boarding school experience at the Carlisle Indian School, and D'Arcy McNickle (Salish/Kootenai). That wave reached a height (that has continued to rise) in 1969 with Kiowa master storyteller N. Scott Momaday's novel *House Made of Dawn*, which won the Pulitzer Prize. The importance of these new keepers of the sacred word is such that I list a number of books and say a few words about them and their authors at the end of each chapter. Through them, as well as through the living oral tradition, our stories are being told.

Perhaps you should think of this book as just another story, a traveler's tale of the sort that occurs in a great many of our cultures. I remember how it was put to me fifteen years ago, when I was in Alaska, by Grace Slwooko, a Siberian Yupik storyteller from St. Lawrence Island, an elderly little woman with so much infectious energy and warmth in her that she literally bounced across the frozen ground as if she were made of rubber. In a number of Yupik and Inupiat communities in Alaska they have what they call the "Longest Story," a tale of travel and adventure that goes on and on and on. As we looked out over the frozen sea in front of Nome, Grace told me how you can sometimes see the mountains of Siberia from her home island. "In the old days," she said, "a young man would take his *umiaq*, his walrus skin boat, and he would paddle across toward those mountains. When he got to shore he would just start walking, maybe for two or three years. When he came back home, he would have enough stories to tell for the rest of his life."

introduction: connections

Recommended Reading

Apess, William (Pequot). *A Son of the Forest* (originally published in 1829). Amherst: University of Massachusetts Press, 1997. This is the first published autobiography of an American Indian. Its author, like a number of educated Indian men of his time, became an ordained minister. Apess fought so vehemently on behalf of Mashpee Indian land claims that many believe his disappearance around 1838 was due to his murder.

Eastman, Charles Alexander, Ohiyesa (Dakota.) *Indian Boyhood* (originally published in 1902). New York: Dover Publications, 1971. This classic story, told by a man who was the most famous Indian writer of the early twentieth century, charts the progression of the narrator's life from his early existence in a Native community through his first encounters with Europeans to his eventual arrival in the world of the white man. Other books by this prolific author, who was one of the founders of the Boy Scouts of America, continued his story. *From the Deep Woods to Civilization* not only tells of his becoming a medical doctor, but also describes how he was one of the first on the scene to treat the survivors of the Wounded Knee Massacre.

La Flesche, Francis (Omaha). *The Middle Five* (originally published in 1900). Lincoln: University of Nebraska Press, 1978. Unlike the other autobiographies on this list, La Flesche's story deals with one part of the author's life, his boarding school experiences.

Standing Bear, Luther (Lakota). *Land of the Spotted Eagle* (originally published in 1933). Lincoln: University of Nebraska Press, 1978. Part of the autobiography of this talented man, who traveled with Buffalo Bill's Wild West Show and became a leading activist for Native rights, deals with his experiences as a member of the first generation of Carlisle students.

Winnemucca, Sarah (Paiute). *Life Among the Piutes* (originally published in 1883). Salt Lake City: University of Utah Press. The first autobiography by an American Indian woman, a Paiute who became a strong and effective advocate for the rights of her people.

doctrine of discovery, native sovereignty, and treaties

My children, when at first I liked the whites,
My children, when at first I liked the whites,
I gave them fruits,
I gave them fruits.

—*Ghost Dance song by Nawat (Arapaho)*

There is a story among the Wabanakis of the North Atlantic Coast that was first told less than five hundred years ago. It is about Glooskap, the powerful being who can change things and defeat monsters. But in the case of this story, the terrible being that threatens the people is the King of France.

"I need trees to build more big ships," the King of France says. "I have cut down all the trees in France. Go find more for me."

So his men sail off to North America, where there are many big trees, and they begin cutting them down. The Wabanakis try to stop these men with hair on their faces because they know that cutting down all the trees is not a good thing. But the hairy-faced Frenchmen have strong weapons and drive the Indians away. So the Indians burn tobacco and pray for help, and Glooskap comes to help them. He is too powerful for the French sailors, and they run away from him, get into their boat—which is so large it looks like a floating island—and then sail away.

Glooskap's grandmother speaks to him. "Grandson," she says, "those hairy-faced people will come back. We must go and see where those strange people came from."

Glooskap says, "We must have a boat like theirs."

So he steps out onto a big stone island in the bay that has tall trees on it. He changes the tall trees on the island into the masts of a ship. He changes the squirrels who are running up and down the tall trees on the island into sailors. He orders the stone island to pull up its roots and float like a canoe and it does so. Then he and his grandmother sail to Europe to confront the King of France and tell him that the Frenchmen do not own the land of the Wabanakis.

When Glooskap arrives on the coast of France late at night, he tells the island to put its roots back down. He changes the masts of his stone ship back into trees and his sailors back into squirrels. The next morning, the King of France looks out and sees the island. He sees the tall trees. He calls his men to him.

"I did not see that island out there in my bay before. It has tall trees on it. Go out and cut them down."

The king's men do as he says. They go out to the island with axes to cut the trees, but Glooskap takes the axes away from them.

"Take my grandmother and me to the one who told you to cut my trees," he says.

So Glooskap is taken to the king.

"Who are you?" says the king. "Why did you stop my men from cutting my trees?"

"They are not your trees," says Glooskap. "They belong to me and my people."

Now the king becomes very angry. He orders his men to beat Glooskap and his grandmother with whips and clubs. But Glooskap just reaches out and takes the whips and clubs away from the men. The king orders his men to tie up Glooskap and his grandmother. But as soon as they are tied, Glooskap just speaks a word and the ropes untie themselves and fall on the ground. The king orders his soldiers to shoot Glooskap and his grandmother. But Glooskap speaks a word and the guns will not fire.

Now the King of France is furious. "Shove them into a cannon," he roars.

So Glooskap and his grandmother are loaded into a cannon. The fuse is lit, there is a great explosion, and when the smoke clears away, all that is left of the cannon is twisted metal, and Glooskap and his grandmother are standing there smoking their pipes.

Now the king understands. He cannot destroy Glooskap and his grandmother.

"The trees of your land belong to you," the King of France says. "I will not take them without your permission."

To understand the complicated relationship between American Indian tribes and the European newcomers, we must look back five centuries. Before 1492, when one nation conquered another in Europe or Asia or Africa, they usually just assumed that the riches of that land belonged to them. Then the Europeans realized that two vast continents existed across the western ocean. Many European nations wanted a part of the wealth of those new lands and a profitable relationship with the millions of American Indians who already lived there. Gaining the wealth of the New World was not the only issue. The European nations, as Christian states, were also concerned with doing things in a way that was in line with the doctrines of the Catholic Church. What rights could Europeans claim in the New World?

Francisco de Vitoria, a respected theologian, was consulted by the King of Spain for his opinion in 1513. In the end, two new ideas were put forth, ideas that were eventually accepted by the other European states. The first was the "doctrine of discovery," which stated that Christian princes discovering new lands had a recognized right to them. Thus it was that one European after another would plant a flag somewhere in America and claim that territory for Spain or France, England or Portugal, Denmark or Germany or Holland. However, it was also decided that only empty land could be claimed outright by such discovery. If there were original inhabitants, then they were the legal owners. Indian land could be taken only with the consent of the aborigines. This was the concept of "Native sovereignty." Unless there was a just war, the Europeans could not simply come in and take over an Indian nation. How could Europeans legally claim Native lands? As Vine Deloria, Jr., explains in *American Indians, American Justice,* in North America they turned to treaty-making. (A treaty is a contract in writing between two or more states or nations.) "The Indian tribes…were recognized," Deloria writes, "as legitimate entities, capable of dealing with the European nations by treaty." Thus it was that this treaty-making "became the basis for defining the legal and political relationships between the Indians and the European colonists."

As soon as the United States came into existence it continued this treaty-making practice. The first U.S. treaty was signed in 1778 with the Delawares. Over the next ninety-three years, 372 treaties were signed between the United States and various Indian nations. There were, quite rightly, many complaints about treaty-making. Treaties were often signed by Indians who were coerced into the agreement or who were not truly the chosen representatives of those whose land they signed away. The treaties were invariably honored by the Indians and broken by the Americans. The last treaty was signed in 1871 with the Nez Perce. Treaty-making was then ended, in part through the efforts of Ely S. Parker, who was not only a Seneca Grand Sachem but also a close friend of President Ulysses S. Grant and the Commissioner of Indian Affairs. Parker had long been disturbed by the inequities in the making of treaties, having seen much of the land of his own Senecas taken through treaties and dishonest land deals.

Although treaty-making ended, the pre-existing treaties still retain legal status. In the last few decades, many of the legal claims filed by Native nations have been based on those treaties, which promised—but never delivered—certain things to Native nations in exchange for land cessions. The recognition of continuing Native sovereignty and the right of recognized Indian tribes to a form of self-government are also based on the principles established through the process that began in 1513. Further, U.S. law established that land sales could be made only through the federal government, by dealing nation to nation, not by states or individuals buying Indian land. Thus, in a number of cases, such as those of the Passamaquoddys and Penobscots of Maine, tribal nations have been able to gain either monetary compensation or the return of some portion of the land that was taken from them in the eighteenth and nineteenth centuries. Indian land claims are still ongoing in the twenty-first century.

the road of stories

MY CHILD, AS YOU TRAVEL ALONG LIFE'S ROAD, NEVER HARM

ANYONE OR CAUSE ANYONE TO FEEL SAD. ON THE CONTRARY,

IF AT ANY TIME YOU CAN MAKE A PERSON HAPPY, DO IT.

—*Anonymous Winnebago speaker, circa 1923*

the journey

ARAPAHO

As we travel, we shall come to four buttes. We must be ready when we come to each of them in turn, for their sides are steep and rocky. If our steps are not careful, we may slip and fall and go no farther. When we reach the top, which is flat and wide, we may stand there and look far in all directions, both behind us and ahead. But, sooner or later, if we would continue, we must climb down the other side. As we pass through the valley between that butte and the next, we are met by White Owl Man. He tests us to see if we remember what we learned from our climb, from what we *saw while we were there on the top, from our experience of leaving that former high place. If we remember all that our past experience taught us, then we are allowed to continue on until we come to the side of the second steep slope. Then we begin the hard climb again.*

So it goes for each of those four buttes in turn. We must make the difficult climb, stand for a time on top seeing far vistas, but then, at last, descend and prepare for yet another ascent.

Each of these four hills has a name. The first is Childhood. The second is Youth. The third is Middle Age. The last is Old Age. That journey which leads us up and down is called the Road of Life.

It often amazes me that, after centuries of continued contact between the indigenous cultures of North America and the descendants of immigrants who now make up the majority of its population, most people in the United States still know very little about the first inhabitants of this continent. This might be more understandable if, as images in the popular media would have us believe, Native Americans were nothing more than violent and disorganized hordes, vanished peoples and cultures who were obliterated by vastly more civilized Europeans. As far as American Indian numbers go, there was, indeed, a long period during which the numbers of indigenous people declined. It was not until as recently as the late nineteenth century that birth rates began to exceed death rates among aboriginal Americans. At the start of the twentieth century, the number of American Indians in the United States was estimated to be as low as 300,000. By the beginning of the twenty-first century, American Indians still represented one of the smaller "ethnic minorities," but we had become one of the fastest-growing populations. On the last United States census rolls of the twentieth century, there were 1,500,000 American Indians.

the road of stories

As far as our cultures and our political organizations—which were many and varied—there was never a lack of sophistication or civilization among the indigenous nations of North America. Nor were the ways of the First Peoples uninfluential. Aboriginal political and military control of vast regions of the continent may now largely be in the past, but the lifeways, philosophies, and indigenous sciences of the First Americans made and continue to make a difference in the development, the very existence, of "America." Through a variety of processes that seem to have gone largely unnoticed, the United States has been shaped by the legacy of its American Indian nations. Yet despite the continuing presence of real Native Americans themselves, that legacy remains largely unrecognized. More than any other people, American Indians are either unnoticed or seen as exotic strangers in their own homelands.

Hearts of Darkness

What are the reasons for this lack of understanding and appreciation? It may partially be a result of that age-old practice (common, it seems, to all nations) of justifying the bad treatment of others by demonizing or dehumanizing them—as the Germans did to the Jews. If Indians were only animals, there was no need to deal fairly with them or even to consider them the rightful owners of land coveted by the newcomers. Natives could be hunted as "vermin," extirpated from land coveted by white settlers and mineral prospectors, as happened in California during the Gold Rush. In fact, Native people were still being hunted like beasts in the late twentieth century in parts of Amazonian South America. (One report in the world press in the 1980s described the trial of a group of Brazilian men who justified killing Indians by claiming that Indians were not human beings.)

Such characterizations of Indians as non-human were backed by the writings of Europeans who, from the sixteenth century on, portrayed not only Native Americans, but Asians, Africans, and Pacific Islanders, as godless, ignorant, cannibalistic savages. That vision of indigenous people as benighted primitives was used by King Leopold II of Belgium to justify his ruthless conquest and colonization of the Congo in Africa at the end of the nineteenth century. Disguising his purely mercenary motives as a desire to end the Arab slave trade, Leopold's reign over the unfortunate Congolese resulted in the deaths of more than eight million Africans. As Jahnheinz Jahn, a twentieth-century German author, put it in the title of his study of the twisted image Europeans created of Africa and Africans, *Wir Nennten Ihn Savagen* (We Named Them Savages). The European colonization of the lands where these "degraded and primitive tribes" lived became not just a good thing, but a blessed enterprise. Bringing the lights of law, reason, and Christianity to these hearts of darkness was a noble endeavor. In the Americas, it also brought the gold and silver of Mexico and Peru back to a Europe that had been in financial collapse, making possible the building of the modern industrial states of the West. In Africa, not only were the mineral wealth and other natural resources torn from the land, but also millions of black slaves, who were shipped to the New World. (It is true that slavery was not introduced to the African continent by Europeans and that the slave factories of the African coast were stocked with Africans primarily captured and sold into slavery by Africans from other tribes who had been seduced by the wealth they could gain as slave providers. However, as I will explain a bit later, the form of slavery used by Europeans to provide slaves for the New World was different from that practiced in Africa and among other indigenous peoples elsewhere in the world.)

It is seldom mentioned in textbooks that slavery in the Americas was not restricted to Africans. Millions of American Indians were taken as slaves. The island of Hispaniola was not only despoiled of its mineral wealth but depopulated by Columbus and his son (who became the first governor of the island) within twenty years of the Genoan explorer's arrival in 1492. Taino Indians were forced into the gold mines, where life expectancy was brutally short and attempts to run away were punished by cutting off an offender's feet. Jack Forbes, a Renape Indian writer, was not being merely ironic when he entitled one of his recent books *Columbus and Other Cannibals*. White indentured servants were also literal slaves in the early years of American colonization. However, runaway indentured servants were able to lose themselves in the European population, and the practice of indenture was gradually replaced by the enslavement of those who did not blend in. Whole Indian nations, starting with the Taino, found themselves pressed into slavery. In seventeenth-century New England, after their military defeat by the English, the survivors of the Narragansett Nation found themselves reduced to servitude to their conquerors.

Slavery, of course, is no new thing. It has been practiced at one time or another in virtually every human society throughout the world, including a number of pre-Columbian American Indian cultures. However, in most of those forms of slavery, slaves were still recognized as human beings and had certain rights. Slaves could marry freely, and the children of slaves were free people, not "born into slavery." Slavery was sometimes only for a set period, to pay off some sort of debt. Whatever a slave owned or produced did not automatically belong to the slave owner.

But the slavery brought to the New World was new. It was chattel slavery, a form of bondage developed by the English in which a human slave had no more rights than a piece of real estate and could be bought and sold as easily as one might sell a wagon or a hoe. There is a paradox to this, that the Indians, who saw this Earth as a living being and showed it the respect one gives one's mother, should find both themselves and their sacred land reduced to the status of property.

In his courageous family chronicle *Slaves in the Family,* John Ball notes the start of this process on his family's lucrative rice plantations when, in 1696, the colonial legislature of South Carolina passed a law asserting chattel status on "All Negroes, Mollatoes [sic], and Indians which at any time heretofor [sic] have been bought and sold." The growing white plantations, farms, and settlements developed a simple, three-fold solution to the problem of Indians who refused to sell their lands: kill them, drive them away, or force them into bondage. A century later, the Tuscaroras of North Carolina were invited to a meeting to discuss land concessions, taken prisoner, and then sold as slaves to the West Indies.

Slavery of American Indians by whites continued well into the nineteenth century in North America—most notably in the Southwest, where it was a major cause of Navajo and Apache resistance against the Spanish and New Mexicans. However, American Indian slavery was never as "successful" as enslaving Africans. Because they were on their own lands, Indians often escaped and could not be recaptured. The rapid Spanish depopulation of the West Indies and the spread of European-introduced epidemics along the continental East Coast also reduced the number of Indians available as slaves. (Microbes were often better soldiers for European colonizers than were men. The conquest of Mexico by Hernan Cortez almost failed when the Aztecs rose up against the conquistadors and drove them out of Mexico City. However, an epidemic of smallpox then weakened the Indians to the point where the returning Spaniards met with little resistance.) The seemingly inexhaustible number of Africans available to the slave trade made black slaves the logical alternative, even though they resisted their masters just as passionately as did American Indians.

One of the great unwritten stories of America is the saga of American Indian and African interaction and cooperation. Local Native American populations gave refuge to runaway African slaves in surprisingly large numbers in the South. The acceptance of those Africans into then racially unprejudiced American Indian cultures throughout North America was so common that the majority of today's African Americans have some measure of American Indian ancestry. Many of the "Maroon" communities of runaway slaves in the American South and South America were a mixture of American Indians and Africans. One of the major reasons the United States waged war on the Seminoles of Florida in the early nineteenth century was to recover the runaway slaves among them. One of the wives of Osceola, the charismatic leader of the Seminole resistance, was an African woman who escaped her captivity.

The Land Is My Blood

While one reason for a lack of understanding between Europeans and American Indians can be traced back to that early insensitivity of Europeans to the humanity of Indians, another reason remains as true today as it was then. It is the European view of the natural world as a resource, its primary value quite simply that of raw material. Indeed, everything that Europe lacked in the way of natural resources could be found in the New World. One small but significant example can be found in the Northeast. Centuries of shipbuilding had wiped out the forests of Europe. (Anyone visiting the dry and rocky islands of Greece might remember that once, long ago, those hills were green and blessed with trees.) In New England, there were great pines perfectly suited for the masts of tall ships. Those trees were so important that the tallest and straightest of them were set aside in the eighteenth century for the British Crown, to be used only for the Royal Navy. The shape of the "King's Arrow" was cut deeply into the trunk of such trees. No unauthorized person might cut such a tree, even if it was on their own land. Those great trees, destined to be used in the building of war ships, were more important than human life.

New England is the homeland of my own *Abenaki* people. Abenaki literally means "Dawn Land," a reference to the fact that our traditional lands, which now are northern New England and the maritime provinces of Canada, are closest to the rising sun. Like the Europeans, my ancestors saw the importance of those ancient trees, as did our neighbors the Iroquois. For the Iroquois the white pines were and still are the visible reminder of the power of peace. For the Abenakis, the great trees are the symbol and the source of human life. The inner bark of the pine can be harvested and ground into a nutritious meal, and its needles can be made into a tea that is good medicine for coughs and colds. Every tree also had its special use in our material culture, a use often reflected in the names given the trees. The birch is the Blanket Tree, for its bark was used to cover our wigwams. The ash is the Snowshoe Tree because its supple wood was easily crafted.

Moreover, Abenakis say that trees are, quite literally, our relatives. Our Creation story tells how human beings were created. Ktsi Nwaskw, the Great Mystery, fired arrows into the trunks of the tall ash trees. Each place where an arrow struck, a man or woman stepped forth. Trees that were mere commodities to Europeans, a means of gaining wealth, were ancestors, deeply felt symbols, life itself to Native people. Trees were acknowledged as living, sentient beings, as were game animals. When they were used, it was because they were needed. Just as the killing of an animal might be followed by thanking its spirit, the cutting of a tree was often preceded by offering thanks. Even when trees were used for timber, as was the case among the Pacific Northwest Coast nations that built great longhouses of cedar planks, the trees might not be killed. Instead, after a ceremony of gratitude, no more would be cut from a living tree than would allow its survival.

It was the same way with the land. Native nations had a sense of ownership when it came to the land, but their understanding was very different from that of Europeans. For example, rather than individual ownership of carefully measured plots of real estate, we Abenakis thought in terms of family hunting areas and territories where our people lived and which we had the right to defend. Giving someone else the right to also live there did not exclude us from continuing to rely on that land for our survival. It was more as if we were owned by the land and were cared for by it. The land was not like an ear of corn or a deerskin or a flint arrowhead, something that could be traded away.

Buying and selling land was the European way, even to the point of selling land thousands of miles away that had always been lived on by other people. To American Indian people, that made no sense. It was not just the illogic of foreign monarchs selling land that they had never seen—as did King James I of England on April 10, 1606, when he signed the royal charter that gave certain British companies the right to settle the huge territory known to the English (but not the indigenous people) as Virginia. The whole idea of selling real estate was unreal to our First Peoples. Their land was sacred earth, not just acreage. In fact, in many of the Native languages of the Americas, the Earth is directly referred to as "Our Mother."

"You ask me to cut grass and make hay and sell it, and be rich like white men?" a Nez Perce religious leader named Smohalla said in 1851. "But how dare I cut off my mother's hair?"

"The soil you see is not ordinary soil—it is the dust of the blood, the flesh, and the bones of our ancestors," said a Crow elder named Curley in 1936. "The land, as it is, is my blood and my dead; and I do not want to give up any portion of it."

From the start, we were speaking different languages in more ways than one. Sometimes it was only through stories that we could make clear what we were really saying. But all too often it seemed that Europeans—and especially their leaders—were both blind and deaf.

The Truth of Our Memories

Indians and European Americans have seldom spoken the same language. More than three hundred languages were spoken by the aboriginal peoples of North America. A great many of those languages are still spoken today, but even in American Indian communities where the indigenous language has vanished or is spoken fluently by a diminishing number of people, the supposedly common language of English often becomes subtly different when it is spoken by American Indians. (This is also true for other European languages. Spanish, as it is spoken by the Native peoples of Central and South America, often takes on certain characteristics of indigenous language structures.)

our stories remember

Whether speaking English or their native languages, Native Americans frequently differentiate between what they know from personal experience, what is general knowledge, and what has been reported to them by someone else. Seventy years ago, when the ethnologist Grenville Goodwin was collecting stories from the White Mountain Apaches, he noted that the word *djindi,* which means "they say" and is used to indicate hearsay, was spoken at the end of each sentence, not only during the telling of tales, but also in conversation when referring to happenings related to the speaker by someone else. When the Lakota elder Black Elk related the story of his life to the poet John Neihardt in 1931, he did so in the presence of other old men who could vouch for his truthfulness. At times, Black Elk turned to one or another of them to relate a particular event because they had experienced it directly, while he had only been told about it. Seven decades later, Hilda Neihardt and Lori Utrecht conducted a series of interviews with the descendants of Black Elk. In the course of their interviews they asked Aaron DeSersa, Jr., the great-grandson of Black Elk who has been entrusted to carry the old man's pipe, about his childhood. His immediate reply was that he could not remember much from when he was small because he had rheumatic fever and so his mother or his aunt should be the ones to talk about it.

The truth of memory is such an important element of discourse that a number of Native languages throughout the Americas make use of suffixes called evidentials. Among the Aymara people of the Andes, for example, there are three different evidentials that may be added to a word to indicate either knowledge acquired through the senses, non-personal knowledge involving the remote past (including history, legends, and myths), and knowledge gained through either written or spoken language. Andean Spanish in the Aymara region now makes those same distinctions.

The homeland of the Cayuga Indians, one of the original Five Nations of the Iroquois League, is in the area now known as the Finger Lakes of New York, far from the mountains of South America. Yet, as with the Aymara language, evidentials are present in the Cayuga language. Thus, when a Cayuga Indian of the seventeenth century heard a white missionary tell the story of how Noah was swallowed by a great fish, the Cayuga man said, "Is that what is said as a story or is that what you know?"

"It is what I know," the missionary replied.

"How many winters have passed since this thing did happen?" the Cayuga man asked.

"More than three thousand winters," the missionary said.

"Is it said to be true that it was that long ago or do you know it to be true?"

"I know it to be true," said the missionary.

As the Cayuga man walked away, he turned to a friend and said, "I know this to be true. Either this white man is a liar or he is much older than he appears to be."

Giving Thanks

Even the simplest words may take on a different meaning because the Native worldview on which the thoughts expressed in English are based is not the same as that of the Western world. This is particularly obvious in the so-called poetic way that American Indian people often express themselves—both in their indigenous language and in whatever European language they speak.

A Mohawk friend of mine, Tom Porter, is a Faithkeeper, an elder charged with certain ceremonial responsibilities. Speaking beautifully and honestly is greatly honored among the Mohawks (and most other American Indian nations). The ability to express oneself with appropriate eloquence and clarity in one's own native language is one of the nearly universal attributes of American Indian leadership. The Iroquois Thanksgiving Address, spoken to open significant occasions, is one example of that sort of eloquent clarity. The form of the Thanksgiving Address is set, with greetings and thanks being given in great detail to the Creator, the Mother Earth, the Waters of the Earth, the Plant beings, and so on, all the way up into the sky, where gratitude is expressed to Elder Brother Sun and Grandmother Moon and Stars. However, each person who is called on to deliver that Thanksgiving Address may do it in his or her own way within that formula—at greater or lesser length. These days, that includes delivering the Thanksgiving first in an Iroquois language and then going through the entire address again in English. It can take a while. Whenever I'm present at an event where an Iroquois speaker stands to give the opening, I always smile when I see white people stand up with him, trying to show their respect, while the Indians in the audience stay seated. It tells me that this is probably the first time for those white folks to hear the address. They don't know what they're in for. I've been present when the Iroquois part of thanking all our relations has taken close to an hour.

In the fall of 2001, the Saratoga Springs Arts Center hosted a multimedia show by Melanie Printup, a Tuscarora artist. Tom Porter was asked to give the opening remarks. Tom began by explaining in English a bit about the way Indians speak.

"Sometimes," Tom said, "people say that the way Indians talk is poetic." He laughed. "I don't understand that—why they say our language is like poetry." He looked out at the audience and, looking at a woman wearing a blue dress, spoke a sentence in Mohawk. "What I have just said might be translated into English that you are wearing a blue dress. But what I actually said in Mohawk is that you are wearing a dress that is the color of the sky." He shifted his gaze to another person and again said something in Mohawk. "I have said that you are wearing clothing that is the color of the grass." Looking at a child, he spoke Mohawk a third time. "And now I have said that you are wearing a shirt which is the same color as the blood, that same blood that flows through our bodies."

Tom nodded once, and then a small smile crossed his face. "I guess that is why they say that we are poetic. It doesn't matter if we are Mohawk or Cheyenne or Navajo—our language is always connected to nature."

People smiled back at Tom. The clarity of his words had touched them. "Now," he said, "I'm going to do the Thanksgiving. I'm not going to do the long form of it. I'm going to keep it short."

And he did. It took him only forty-five minutes. Some of the white folks were still standing when he was done.

The language diversity of the Western Hemisphere before European colonization was truly impressive. Perhaps one-third of all the world's languages were found here. Shirley Silver and Wick R. Miller, the authors of *American Indian Languages: Cultural and Social Contexts,* estimate that more than 750 languages existed in North America while another 500 languages were spoken in South America. Silvan and Miller note than an unnamed European observer in 1590 stated that "they speak so many languages, so different from each other" that "in many provinces one doesn't go a league without coming across another language, as remote and distinct from the first as Castilian Spanish is from Basque, or from English, or from African languages."

None of these indigenous languages were related to the languages of Europe. There are no European languages based on polysynthesis, a process of word formation that results in long single words embodying notions that would be an entire sentence in a language such as English. Many, though not all, American Indian languages are polysynthetic, including the Algonkian languages of the East Coast that were among the first encountered by the European colonists of North America. The frequent use of glottalized consonants (a consonant voiced with a distinctive popping sound at the end) found in many American Indian languages was extremely strange to the ears of the European newcomers. Because these languages were so different, some early European writers looked down upon the indigenous tongues of the Americas as primitive or not "real" human speech. However, those who closely studied those languages—such as the Jesuit missionaries—recognized, even early on, how varied, sophisticated, and well developed those languages were. There is no one "typical" American Indian language, just as there is no one indigenous culture in the Western Hemisphere that could be said to represent everything about American Indians, or one American Indian who speaks for all Natives past and present. Nevertheless, Tom Porter's statement about our languages always connecting us to nature is one generalization that seems to hold true. Our languages and our stories hold those ancient ties.

American Indian cultures, as a whole, have been deeply connected to nature, not just through language but through custom, tradition, ceremony, and—even more important—self-awareness. The religious traditions and the languages of the Western world have a good part of their roots in nature, but those roots have become attenuated or cut off. The most common stance in the West is that human beings are above nature, superior, paragons, holding dominion. The self-awareness of a western man (I purposely chose the masculine gender) is that of the rugged individual. In America, it is the self-made man, the perception (whether it is true or not) that any man can be powerful or famous or president or a millionaire. It may explain why so many billions of dollars are spent on lottery tickets by the poorest among us. Nature, the Earth, the birds, and the animals are either natural resources meant to be conserved for our use, or nuisances to be bulldozed, shot, poisoned, and removed.

The Place of Stories

Symbols. Images. Ways of seeing.

In every possible medium, from sculpture and painting to music, literature, film, and television, our peoples have been depicted by non-Indians. Innumerable stories have been told about us that bear little or no resemblance to the true realities of American Indian life—past or present. So much so that even Indians may sometimes be confused about themselves, especially when our own stories and traditions, our family structures, and even our original languages have been denied to us.

the road of stories

Perhaps then, in the long run, it is only through our own stories that people—Indian and non-Indian alike—can begin to understand the true American Indian heritage. Stories have always been at the heart of all our Native cultures. Although they have been classified as myths and legends, or placed under the rubric of oral traditions, these powerful tales are not just spoken or written words to American Indian people. They are alive. Alive as breath and the wind that touches every corner of this land. Alive as memory, memory that shapes and explains a universe, alive, aware, and filled with power. Our stories open our eyes and hearts to a world of animals and plants, of earth and water and sky. They take us under the skin and into the heartbeat of Creation. They remind us of the true meaning of all that lives. Our stories remember when people forget.

What is the place and purpose of stories? What is their proper use? Stories were never "just a story," in the sense of being merely entertainment. They were and remain a powerful tool for teaching. Lesson stories were used by every American Indian nation as a way of socializing the young and strengthening the values of their tribal nation for both young and old. In almost every American Indian nation, there were different classes of stories—such as the stories of creation, stories relating historical events, and narratives of personal experience. There were often certain times and places appropriate for stories, especially those of the ancient times when the Earth was being created and the animals were in the form of people.

Frequently, such stories could be told only in the winter time or at night. To tell these stories at the wrong time would bring unfortunate consequences to the teller. They would not be punished by any human agency, but by the natural world itself. Among the Iroquois, it is said that snakes will enter the house of a person who tells a restricted story in the summer. The Abenakis say that a bee may sting the offending storyteller on the lips. In the Southeast, among the Natchez, the Creeks, and many other peoples, stories were to be told only at night and after the coming of the first frost. The Pueblo nations, who stress the importance of stories as guides for behavior, typically relate their stories in their homes on winter nights. The Modocs and Wintuns of California stress that myth-telling in the summer attracts Rattlesnake, while the Yuroks say that storytellers who recount traditional tales during the daylight hours will become hunchbacked. White Mountain Apache tales are also to be told during the night, when Sun cannot see you, during the coldest months—from November through February. That way, such great dangers as lightning, poisonous snakes, and biting insects, all of which sleep during the winter, would not know their names had been spoken and come to take revenge. Stories such as that of the contest between the animals of the day and the animals of the night, the Chiricahua Apaches explain, must be told only on winter nights. Otherwise the animals of the losing side— such as Snake and Bear—will take revenge on the teller and his family.

"If you talk about Coyote at the wrong time or even mention his name," a Pueblo friend of mine said a few years ago, "we say that Coyote may come and visit you and bring trouble." Words and names are such powerful things that many tribal nations avoid saying the names of certain powerful, potentially dangerous creatures—such as Bear or Coyote—but refer to them indirectly and respectfully. Navajo names for Bear include "Fine Chief" and "The One Who Lives in a Den," while the Crees of the far north refer to Bear as "Four-Legged Human" and "Chief's Son." The Kwakiutls of the Pacific Northwest address the bear as "Supernatural One," and the Mahicans of the eastern woodlands call Bear "Grandfather."

Ordinary stories, including tales of personal experience, usually did not have such restrictions and could be told at any time. Making reference to the myths and even the quoting of fragments from them might also be used to teach important lessons at any time. Further, throughout Native North America, stories were usually not told exactly the same and word for word every time. (There were, of course, sacred formulas that did have to be memorized word for word. The most vivid examples of such unvarying sacred texts are the "Ways," healing chants done by a Diné, *hataaχii,* a medicine man or singer. Some of these healing chants, such as the Night Way or the Shooting Way, may take several days, and they must be done exactly the same every time. Otherwise, the deities whose presence is being solicited by that chant will fail to appear and heal the patient. It may take years for a *hataaχii* to learn one chant.) The framework of the story stayed the same, but each storyteller filled in as he or she saw necessary. Even the same teller might tell the same story a little differently depending on the audience and the point that he or she wanted to make. I know of occasions when two different storytellers from the same tribal nation have told the same story and then discussed with each other about whose version was more correct.

To our people, our stories are alive and we are part of our stories. There is a wonderful afterword by the Western Shoshone storyteller Beverly Crum in *Shoshone Myths.* She describes the live and lively setting when stories were told (as opposed to the "isolating experience" of seeing stories on paper), the way members of her family responded, asked questions, and made comments during the telling of one of those familiar and powerful tales of the old times. "Sometimes," she said, "my father would interrupt my mother, if she were telling a story, to add a phrase or song she might have forgotten. My mother did the same thing when my father told a story."

The important role that stories played and continue to play in American Indian communities can be seen by considering the place stories held and still hold in the lives of the Western Apaches. In the old days, stories were just as important as shelter building, hunting, and ceremonies. They taught people about every aspect of the world and also showed the right way to behave. Coyote stories showed children the consequences of wrong actions, while funny stories and stories about otherwise taboo topics provided them with what the anthropologist Morris Opler called a "cultural safety valve." Of course, Coyote is more than just a safety valve. After all, he can change himself into just about anything he wants to be, and he always has more to say about everything. Rest assured—or be warned—you'll be running into him again in later chapters.

our stories remember

In his 1993 preface to the reissue of Grenville Goodwin's *Myths and Tales of the White Mountain Apache,* White Mountain Tribal Chairman Ronnie Lupe was not talking about the past when he said that their stories tell people "how to act and why." If someone misbehaves, a story is "shot like an arrow at a family member whose conduct has been inappropriate, and the person is guided back to the path of correct Apache behavior."

What about the use of our stories by non-Indians? What about professional storytellers who get paid to tell a tale or people writing books? These are questions worth asking, especially at a time when the important issue of the intellectual property rights of Native peoples has finally been raised. In the past, viewing oral tradition as "uncopyrightable," non-Indians have frequently used our stories in ways that Indians see as inappropriate. Ever since the eighteenth century, plays, novels, stories, and books for children have been written by non-Indians using American Indian sources. The twentieth century brought the new media of radio, movies, television, and video games. In some ways, you could say that Indians were central to the birth of the motion-picture industry. An incredible number of films have been made about Indians, from Edison's first kinetoscopes in 1894 to *Dances with Wolves* in 1990. More than one hundred movies about Indians were released in 1910 alone, according to Michael Hilger in *The American Indian Film.* The image of the Plains Indian on horseback has been seen in every country in the world to the point where it is the image of a "real Indian" in international popular culture.

Even now, despite the fact that we have a highly talented and prolific new generation of American Indian authors writing their own books, the vast majority of new "American Indian" books appearing in print each year are written by white people. Sometimes the published material is accurate. Sometimes, in the tradition of Henry Wadsworth Longfellow's nineteenth-century epic poem *The Song of Hiawatha,* it draws on real traditions but makes big mistakes. Sometimes, especially in the case of writers who make American

Indian spirituality their New Age focus, these books are inaccurate to the point of the blasphemous and the ridiculous, especially when these writers spin out long yarns about their secret initiations into Native American mysteries by mysterious shamans and powerful medicine people (none of whom appear to have left a forwarding address so that anyone else can find them) who appear to have been holding their breath just waiting for the right white person to come along. Sometimes (and this has happened to me on a number of occasions) someone takes a story told (or even published!) by a Native author, "retells" it (including details that are not traditional, but totally original to that Native writer), and then publishes it under his or her own name.

There are, I believe, a couple of simple rules that should be followed by non-Native people in their use of our stories.

The first is to accept the fact that Native people do have the right to their own traditions. This means that the first people to turn to about a story are the Native people themselves. It also means that you have a responsibility to obtain permission to use that story if you are a writer or a professional storyteller. (I do not include teachers in this category if they are using material in their classrooms from books written by American Indian writers. I have been told by every American Indian writer I know that they welcome such use of their work in classrooms. That is why they wrote their books—for them to be read and well used.) Connected to the issue of permission is the author's and storyteller's responsibility to give something back in return for what they have been given. It may mean sharing royalties or making a commitment to support a Native community in various ways. Let your heart and your honor show you the way.

The second is, once again, to remember always that there is not one overall American Indian culture. There are many. When talking about an American Indian story you need to be specific about what particular Native nation owns that story. Always acknowledge the nation and the individual or individuals who have shared that story. Remember, too, that stories are embedded in a cultural matrix. Every story lives within the larger circle of a nation, and there are aspects of the story that can be understood only by knowing more than the story tells on its surface. Aaron DeSersa, Jr., is a Lakota pipe carrier who is the great-grandson of Nicholas Black Elk. He spoke these words while being interviewed for the book *Black Elk Lives*:

> Book learning is not everything. Words—you can read a book, and you think you understand it, but the living of that life is different. No matter what the book says, living the life, all your life, all we do, is completely different.

If your only knowledge about a story is from a book, acknowledge that fact. Be honest. And, in line with that suggestion, be prepared to hear and accept the word "no." Asking permission to make use of something does not automatically guarantee that you will be allowed to. Some stories are deeply personal, sacred, or restricted in some fashion. When Albert White Man, a Cheyenne traditional dancer from the Northern Cheyenne Reservation, taught me how to tell the Cheyenne story of the coming of the Grass Dance, he told me that I could tell that story only before someone was going to do the Grass Dance. That was more than a decade ago. I have told that story only once since then—at a powwow just before a Grass Dancer entered the circle. Rather than feeling limited, I regard myself as having been honored by being trusted in that way. However, there are also stories that I have heard and I will not tell or write down because I have been told to keep them in my heart.

Perhaps you might think of it this way. We live within the circle of life. That which shapes the circle around us is made up of things that we see and things that we do not see, things that we may describe and things that are beyond all of our powers of description. It is also made up of those things that we may do and those that we may not do. *Yes* and *no* each has its place in the shaping of that circle. If we wish that circle to remain unbroken, we must honor every part of it. And so it is with our stories. The stories are a road that always circles back again. The stories are our breath, that life-giving cycle that flows from our mouths to be shared by the air and then is carried back to us again by the wind.

Recommended Reading

Neihardt, Hilda, and Utrecht, Lori. *Black Elk Lives: Conversations with the Black Elk Family*. Lincoln: University of Nebraska Press, 2000. This is a marvelous continuation of the story of Black Elk, the famous Lakota holy man, as well as a testament to the enduring power of sacred traditions.

Ortiz, Simon J. (Acoma Pueblo). *Woven Stone*. Tucson: University of Arizona Press, 1998. Ortiz has long been both a uniquely Native voice in American poetry and one of the most popular writers among other Indians. This book brings together several of his volumes of personal, narrative, deeply felt poetry.

Silko, Leslie Marmon (Laguna Pueblo). *Storyteller*. New York: Norton, 1977. Silko's novel *Ceremony* is one of the most highly praised works of American Indian fiction, but this out-of-print collection is equally moving and significant. The place of stories in Silko's own life is made clear in her wonderful pieces of short fiction and incisive personal essays.

Velarde, Pablita (Santa Clara Pueblo). *Old Father Storyteller*. Taos, New Mexico: Clear Light Publishing, 1960. Pablita Velarde was best known as an influential figure in American Indian art, but this volume, beautifully illustrated with her paintings, shows that she was also gifted with the true voice of a storyteller.

time line:
development of native american art
in north america

In creating a time line that indicates when certain kinds of Native American art originated, some dates remain inexact. Written records did not exist for most American Indian cultures prior to the sixteenth century except for the peoples of Central America. Certain arts—such as pottery and the carving of bone and stone—are very ancient. Those objects have survived for thousands of years buried in the earth. Works of art made from leather, bark, and wood were also probably made thousands of years ago, but such things do not last as long as stone or bone. We do know when certain innovations were introduced after the coming of Europeans. Steel tools, for example, produced new forms of and changes in American Indian art.

Further, Native American art was generally not viewed as art until the late nineteenth and early twentieth century, when people first began to respect the cultures of American Indians and view their artworks as something more than primitive crafts.

The following time line is not complete but provides some key dates and time frames, with an emphasis on modern developments in American Indian art.

- **More than 10,000 years ago:**
  - petroglyphs made on exposed rocks throughout North America (e.g., Newspaper Rock in Arizona)
  - flintnapping of projectile points and other shapes in stone
  - carvings made of stone and bone throughout the continent, including effigy pipes and lifelike figures of animals, birds, and people
  - pottery made by the method of coiling clay, smoothing with fingers or a paddle, and firing in a pit

- **More than 1,000 years ago:**
  - birch bark and other barkwork—basketry, incising shapes and symbols in bark, making decorated canoes
  - making and stringing of shell beads to create mnemonic records (wampum) and jewelry
  - mural painting in the kivas (Pueblo sacred ceremonial structures) and on canyon walls in the Southwest for religious purposes
  - painted house posts and totem poles depicting ancestral figures and legendary events carved from cedar by various Native tribes of the Pacific Northwest

- **15th or 16th century:** Navajo sand paintings probably originate at this time

- **17th century:** silver and other metal-smithing introduced to northeastern and southeastern tribes

- **1830s:** ledger book art beginning among the Mandans of North Dakota

- **1875:** Plains Indians taken as prisoners to Fort Marion in Florida; supplied with paper, pencils, ink, and paints by Lieutenant Richard Henry Pratt; and begin to develop their own painting styles based on the pictographic tradition, signing their pictures

- **1880s:** American Indians in the Southwest begin putting art on paper with crayons and paint

- **late 19th century until 1934:** U.S. Government forbids teaching American Indians about their arts and Native heritage

- **circa 1928:** Kiowa Five (five Kiowa boy painters) accepted for training at Oklahoma University; Santa Fe Indian School Studio, under Dorothy Dunn, opens classes for American Indian artists from tribes throughout the United States

- **1934:** ban on teaching American Indian arts lifted as part of the Indian Reorganization Act

- **1962:** Institute of American Indian Arts (IAIA) founded in New Mexico

- **1960s:** Pueblo storyteller dolls made of pottery originate among the Pueblos

- **1989:** legislation passed in Congress to establish the National Museum of the American Indian (NMAI), with sites in New York City (Heye Center Museum in the old customshouse in lower Manhattan, opened in 1994); Suitland, Maryland (NMAI Cultural Resources Center, opened in 1994); and Washington, D.C. (the major museum site for NMAI on the Mall, slated for completion around 2004)

who are we?

YOU LOOK AT ME AND YOU SEE ONLY AN UGLY OLD MAN,

BUT WITHIN I AM FILLED WITH GREAT BEAUTY. I SIT AS ON A

MOUNTAINTOP AND LOOK INTO THE FUTURE. I SEE MY PEOPLE

AND YOUR PEOPLE LIVING TOGETHER.

—Sandoval, Hastin Tlo'tsi Hee/

Old Man Buffalo Grass (Navajo), 1928

great hare makes the people

(POWHATAN)

Great Hare lives in his home in the sunrise. There he made the first women and men. He kept them at first in a great bag. It was well that he did so, for the Four Wind Giants smelled those first women and men and came howling to the lodge of Great Hare. The Wind Giants were then much as they are now, without shape or form, but with the power to knock down great trees and fly through the air with a sound so great that it is frightening.

In they came, roaring in from each of the directions, from the Winter Land, the Sunrise Land, the Land of Summer, and the Dark Land.

"We are hungry," the Four Wind Giants howled. "Open your bag. Give us those new ones you have made. Open your bag so we can get at them. We will eat them."

Great Hare, though, was not frightened. "No," he said. "Go away."

And the Four Wind Giants did just that.

After Great Hare drove the Four Wind Giants away, he made the waters and in those waters, placed the fish. Thus there would be food in the waters for the people. Great Hare made the plants of the Earth and on the Earth he placed a Great Deer. Great Deer walked about on the Earth feeding upon those plants as Great Hare intended.

The Four Wind Giants were still angry because Great Hare had not allowed them to eat the first people. They saw what Great Hare had done. It made them even more jealous. So those Four Wind Giants came flying back from their homes in the four directions. They made spears from sharp poles. They hunted the Great Deer and killed it with their spears. They cut it into pieces and ate it, leaving nothing but the hairs of the deer scattered upon the ground. Then the Four Winds once more went away.

Great Hare saw what the Four Wind Giants had done. He gathered up all of the hairs of the Great Deer. Then Great Hare began to speak powerful words; he began to chant and sing. As he sang and chanted, he scattered the hairs of Great Deer on the Earth. Each hair, when it struck the Earth, turned into a deer and ran away into the forest. So it is that there are many deer to this day.

Now that Great Hare had placed the deer all throughout the land, he decided it was time to also release the people, for they could hunt the deer and thus survive on their own. So Great Hare opened his bag. Within that bag there were now many men and women. With care, Great Hare took them from his bag two by two. He placed a Woman and a Man in one country, then he placed another Woman and

Man in another country, and so on, until there were people in every country. Those first people were the ancestors of all of us.

Who Are You?

There has been a long debate among white scientists about the origins of the Native peoples of the two continents that became known as the Americas. Were we survivors of the sunken continents of Mu or Atlantis? Were we the descendants of Egyptians or the Lost Tribe of Israel? Or did our ancestors following migratory herds of game animals simply wander over a long-vanished land bridge between Siberia and Alaska in the region of the Bering Strait?

Preposterous as some of those ideas may sound now, at various points in the eighteenth, nineteenth, and twentieth centuries each of those theories was taken quite seriously. There are still people who speak with great conviction of "Chariots of the Gods," ancient spaceship visits to America by extraterrestrial beings. Advanced "alien science" explains such things as the Nazca lines, those giant geoglyphs carved into the earth of the dry Andean highlands, or the pyramids of Central America (that is, if Egyptians didn't build them). Were some of our forebears aliens? Are the Mayans really from Mars? Are Kiowas related to Klingons? (I can already hear the heavy footsteps of certain Kiowa friends coming after me for that remark!) Who are we and where did we come from?

Before I go further into the history of how Europeans have struggled to explain our origins, let me turn things around for a moment and look through our eyes instead. I'll begin, as the day begins.

Awani gi ya? That is how we say "Who are you?" in the Abenaki language. Because of our geographic location in the Northeast, our Dawn Land ancestors were among the first Indians to discover Europeans on our shores. Long before

Columbus, some of our stories tell us, men came from the direction of the sunrise and stayed for a time. Some Native traditions, among the Micmacs in Canada, for example, seem to indicate the arrival of Europeans in Nova Scotia well before Columbus. Perhaps they refer to the Lord Sinclair expedition that his descendants claim was successful in reaching Newfoundland and Nova Scotia a century before Columbus, guided by Basque navigators. Or they may keep the memory of the now-documented Norse voyage and short period of settlement in North America seven hundred years before that. After decades of debunking supposed Viking sites in New England, "runestones" in the Great Lakes region, and American Indian traditions about such visitors to the coast of northeastern Canada, conclusive proof was found in L'Anse aux Meadows (a corruption of L'Anse aux Meduse, Jellyfish Creek) in Newfoundland that a Norse settlement existed for at least a brief time five centuries before Columbus. A Norwegian history buff named Helge Ingstad and his archaeologist wife, Anne Stine Ingstad, successfully excavated eight Viking houses at L'Anse aux Meadows that dated from about 1000 A.D. In 1978, the area was declared a World Heritage Site by UNESCO.

Considering the currents and the string of islands that a small boat can stop at along the way, it may have been possible for Irish monks to also make that journey from the westernmost British Isles. The voyage of St. Brendan in a skin boat was duplicated with relative ease in recent years by an adventurer named Tim Severin, who tells his story in *The Brendan Voyage*. Long before our land was renamed New England, strange people came to visit us.

Dawn Land and New England. The Native name for our place and the English name offer an interesting contrast in the way the land is seen in relation to the people. In English, places are often named for people, as the modern map of New England attests. *England* comes from "Angle Land," the "Land of the English." But *Dawn Land* comes from the light of dawn, from the place itself. There is a great difference in worldview between those who name a place for themselves and those who name themselves for an aspect of nature. If we translate the old Native names that are still found on the modern maps of America and the names by which many American Indian tribal nations are still known, and contrast them with the new European-derived names, that difference becomes very evident. Connecticut comes from the Abenaki word that means "At the Long River," whereas Delaware comes from the name of Lord Delaware, one of the wealthy and noble English founders of the colony. Pennsylvania, which means "Penn's Woods," memorializes William Penn (confronted with the possibility of leaving one's name on the land, even a Quaker could give in to vanity). New York and New Jersey both bring English names to North America.

I was told a story once by Stephen Laurent, an Abenaki elder. His father, Joseph Laurent, a former chief of the Abenakis of Odanak, was the author of an Abenaki grammar book, and Stephen carried on his dad's lifelong love of our native tongue. Abenaki is like other Algonkian languages in that it can create new words by linking existing words together in a way that describes something new to us.

"When the Europeans first appeared," Stephen said, "we needed to make a new word to call these newcomers. So we observed them carefully. We saw that they wore thick coats and never took them off, even when it was so hot that they were covered with sweat." As a result of that, some peoples of the East Coast ended up calling Europeans "Coatmen," as did the Narragansetts.

"Those new people also never seemed to want to bathe. As a result, they smelled bad." This is not an exaggeration. Bathing was regarded as unhygienic by Europeans until well into the nineteenth century. The early white colonists wore the same clothing without changing it for very long periods of time. It would come to be said by American Indian peoples all over the continent that you could usually smell a white man coming well before you saw him. One of the first things done when white people were taken captive was to make them bathe and then put on new clothing. This was such a transforming experience for some white people that, as Titus King—a white man taken captive by the Abenakis in the eighteenth century—put it, he "began to feel like he was an Indian."

"The faces of the whites were also strange to look at, as hairy as the faces of squirrels," continued Stephen. In those days it was common for most white men to wear beards. It is true that Europeans tend to have more body and facial hair than American Indians, but it is not true that Indians had no hair at all on their faces. The widespread custom, throughout the Americas, is for men to pluck out their facial hair. The faces of the Europeans were amazingly hairy—furry as the face of Raccoon or Bear. To top it off, some of them also had no hair at all on top of their head. Because of this tendency toward male pattern baldness accompanied by a thick beard, white people were given the name "Upside-down Face" by some of the Indian nations of the Pacific Northwest.

"In addition to their appearance, these new people behaved very strangely. When we welcomed them as guests, they responded by taking our people captive or killing us with their strange weapons that roared like thunder.

"Seeing how strangely they looked and acted," Stephen Laurent concluded, "our Abenaki people came up with a name for the whites. It is Awani geek nee geek. It means 'Who are these people?'"

Histories and Our Stories

The question of when the first American Indians reached this continent is an even more controversial topic now than it was a hundred years ago. By the start of the twentieth century it had been well established in the minds of the scientific community that North and South America had been first settled during the period when the glaciers receded from the northern part of the Western Hemisphere, about 10,000 years ago. After that time, they theorized, nomadic hunters crossed the Bering Strait from Siberia and gradually settled the entirety of the New World. The scientists based their conclusions on carefully studied archaeological sites, the dispersal and changes in American Indian languages, and such "racial characteristics" as the shape of teeth and "Mongoloid features," which indicated Asian origin.

our stories remember

Those theories replaced, though not in less scientific circles, the belief that American Indians were in fact the descendants of that wandering Lost Tribe of Israel that left the Middle East, found their way across the Atlantic, and settled in America. That view was bolstered in such books as James Adair's *History of the American Indians,* published in London in 1775. Adair admired, even loved, the Indians of the South, especially the Chickasaws and Cherokees. After many years of living among them and studying their languages and their stories, he concluded that substantial remnants of both Hebrew language and culture remained among the Cherokees. Unfortunately for his theories, Adair did not take into account the fact that his Cherokee informants told him stories in Cherokee that closely paralleled the events in the first five books of the Bible because those same Bible stories had been told to their families by white missionaries. They knew such tales would interest their inquisitive friend. After all, a good story bears repeating.

Just as Adair's theories are now discounted, so, too, the idea that human beings found their way to the Americas only 10,000 years ago is being seriously challenged. A number of archaeological sites in both North and South America have been authenticated to be considerably older than that interglacial period 10,000 years ago. The date of the "first man" in North America, some scientists now believe, may have been 25,000 years ago, or 50,000 years ago, or more. To make things even more interesting, the 10,000-year-old skeletal remains of a man—dubbed "Kennewick man"— found in the Pacific Northwest have been identified by some members of the scientific community as not American Indian or Asian, but Caucasian.

Uncertain and changeable as European scientists and theorists may have been about Native origins, there was no doubt on our parts about who we were or where we came from. Native tradition—a word I prefer to use rather than myth or legend, since both those words imply fanciful untruth—links our origins to the American soil. Here in North America, on Turtle Island, we had our genesis. Story after story tells of our being shaped from this earth. At the very least, unless we are talking about the northernmost peoples of the American continent—the Inuits who have been going back and forth between Asia and North America for centuries—any "migration"s to North America happened much longer than 10,000 years ago. Much, much longer. We are not just from this land, our stories tell us, we are this land. And the land continues to make us. As Oren Lyons, an Onondaga Faithkeeper, once said to me, "We see the faces of our children yet to be born, just there beneath the soil."

The truth of such stories is, I know, an issue here for the literal-minded. Symbolic truth, truth explained through the formula of carefully remembered and often repeated stories, characterizes American Indian histories. Some parts of those stories might be labeled fiction and others fact by a non-Indian listener, but for the Native person, truth is neither so elusive nor so painfully literal. Being able to think in metaphor and to see the spirit that exists in all things may be a necessary requirement for the kind of relationships that American Indian people have to their traditional stories, relationships wrongly interpreted by Europeans as ignorant and credulous.

One of the most common modern views of the universe is that it is a great mechanism. The work of such great scientists and philosophers as Galileo and Copernicus led to the modern replacement of God with Science. Things happen because of scientific principles explained through mathematics, biology, and physics, not because of the workings of an all-powerful deity. Although this is an oversimplification, it could be said that in terms of the workings of the natural world, the Western mind believes that everything can be explained through theory—a formula, proposition, or statement based in logic deduced from a set of axioms.

To say that, on the other hand, the Native peoples of the Americas were unaware of any sort of science would be both incorrect and in line with the sort of superior attitude toward "primitive cultures" that characterized the Indian policies of the United States governments from the eighteenth century through the twentieth. Native peoples of Central America, such as the Mayans, were astronomers and mathematicians of a very high order. Earthworks and structures all over the American continents are now being recognized as not just ceremonial centers, but also highly accurate calendar devices. However, any American Indian knowledge of mathematics and scientific principles did not result in the loss or replacement of spiritual belief. Rather than a mechanistic world, the world of the Native American peoples is a world that is alive. Though they might have independently invented the concept of zero and found ways to make sophisticated calculations, the Mayans saw the very numbers themselves as living beings. Whereas in the Western mind everything has a theory, in the American Indian mind everything has a story. And those stories themselves, rather than just being combinations of spoken or written words, are alive.

As I mention in my introduction to this book, repetition is one of the time-honored devices for learning among American Indians, so let me reiterate that our stories always serve at least two purposes. They are told for the sake of entertainment itself (helping us, as Maurice Dennis, an Abenaki elder, put it to me, "survive another winter") and because that which is entertaining will be listened to and remembered. The second purpose of stories is to teach, to educate about things one needs to know, to guide people toward proper behavior, to show the results of good behavior, to warn about the consequences of ill-considered or selfish actions. It was that way; it is still that way. And one story always leads to another.

who are we?

Recommended Reading

Deloria, Vine, Jr. (Lakota). *Red Earth, White Lies.* Golden, Colo.: Fulcrum Publishing, 1997. The migration, some 10,000 years ago, of our ancestors over the Bering Land Bridge is only one of the theories challenged in this thought-provoking and often bitingly amusing book by one of Native America's brightest and most iconoclastic essayists.

Francis, Lee (Laguna Pueblo). *Indian Time.* New York: St. Martin's Press, 1996. This is the most thorough, readable, and interesting chronology of the Native peoples and cultures of North America that has yet been published. It is a wonderful catalogue of the history, art, legends, literature, philosophy, wisdom, and heroes of Native America from the distant past to the end of the twentieth century.

ceremony

Beauty before me I walk
beauty below me I walk
beauty all around me I walk
in beauty all is restored
in beauty all is made whole…

—*from the Diné "Nightway"*

"Every morning when I get up to get a drink of water from the sink, I always remember to thank the water." Those words were spoken to me thirty years ago by Dewasentah, an Onondaga Clan Mother who was always reminding me of the sacred relationship that exists between all things and the responsibility we humans have to acknowledge that relationship.

One of the ways that relationship is expressed in American life is through what Europeans call ceremony. The dictionary defines *ceremony* as a formal act or series of acts performed solemnly as prescribed by ritual or tribal procedure. Although that is certainly true, it can also be said that, for American Indian people, ceremony is life itself. Tom Porter, a Mohawk elder, told me that one reason why we have so many ceremonies is that humans are forgetful. If we just remembered to give thanks every day and then behave in a thankful and respectful manner, that would be enough. But each time we forget, we need to be given more ceremonies to help us remember.

American Indian ceremonial practices can be as simple as the offering of tobacco with a prayer or as complex as the healing traditions of the Diné. Those traditions, known as "Ways," involve a highly trained *hataaXii*, or "chanter," who has spent years memorizing the words and the protocol for one or more of those Ways, each of which is used for a particular healing purpose. The most common, Blessingway, is often used to restore physical and spiritual balance in an individual. Enemyway is used for a Diné person who has been in battle and touched an enemy, thus causing a spiritual imbalance. For the healing, a dry painting is created on the ground using colored sand and pieces of ground-up bark. This sand painting is a mandala that depicts some event from the Diné Creation Story, perhaps the victory of the Hero Twins over a monster. The person to be healed is seated on the painting as the *hataaℷii* chants the particular Healing Way. These Ways may take several days to complete. Because the presence of others who wish to offer their support makes the Healing Way more successful, many people are invited to attend.

Even events that are viewed as nothing more than games are often part of Native ceremonial practice. One example of this is the American Indian game now known as lacrosse. Called *Tewaarathon* in Mohawk, it is the "Great Game" or the "Creator's Game." When it was played, the field might have been miles in length, and the entire population of one or more villages might have taken part. Such games were usually played to help restore the health of a person to whom the game was dedicated. When the Iroquois prophet Handsome Lake became ill on his final visit to the Onondaga Nation in 1815, a game of lacrosse was immediately planned and played in an attempt to bring healing to the mortally ill elder. (Although he was not cured, he responded to the honor they gave him by saying, "I will soon go to my new home. Soon I will step into the new world, for there is a plain pathway leading me there.")

Some of the best-known ceremonies among Native people have been either sensationalized or misinterpreted. The potlatch ceremonies found among many of the Native peoples of the Pacific Northwest have been referred to as "fighting with wealth" by anthropologists who describe potlatch ceremonies in which a prominent figure tries to outdo a rival by either giving away or destroying vast amounts of personal possessions. The Canadian government and the U.S. Bureau of Indian Affairs were both so alarmed by their perception of potlatches as wasteful that potlatches were outlawed for much of the twentieth century. Although potlatches were, indeed, ostentatious affairs used to build or restore prestige, there was more to them than Europeans understood. *Potlatch* itself comes from the Nootka word *patshatl,* which means "giving." It could be said that while the accumulation of personal wealth is a desirable social norm in mainstream American culture, just the opposite is true in American Indian cultures. Sitting Bull, the great Lakota leader, once said that his people loved him because he was so poor.

The tradition of the giveaway as a ceremony to give thanks by showing great generosity is widespread throughout Native North America. I know of a Cheyenne family in Montana who promised to do a big giveaway if their son returned safely from Vietnam. All the while he was gone, they accumulated huge amounts of things to give away—blankets, canned goods, all kinds of things. When he returned home safely, their giveaway took place. Not only did they give away everything they'd gotten together, but also they were so happy that they gave away their refrigerator, their television, their record player, their radio, their pickup truck, and all their own clothing. Finally, they signed away the deed to their house. They not only showed how great their love was for their son, how truly grateful they were to Maheo, the Great Mystery, but they also made a great name for themselves in their community. Though they were now poor, they were rich in the eyes of their people.

At its best, a potlatch was a way to redistribute material wealth, rather than leaving it in the hands of a few. The imbalance of potlatches in the late 1800s, at which blankets and other goods were not just given away, but burned, seems to have resulted from the influx of European goods and the potential to accumulate excessive wealth on the part of those who traded with the whites. Today, the potlatch has been restored in many of the Northwest tribal nations as a ceremony to give thanks and gain honor by giving.

Ceremony reminds us, through song, story, dance, and dress, through ritual behavior and sacrifice, that we are one with everything around us. To be in balance within ourselves and with that world around us is the proper and natural way. Through ceremony, we may both acknowledge and restore that balance.

origins

THE EARTH IS THE MOTHER OF ALL PEOPLE

AND ALL PEOPLE SHOULD HAVE EQUAL RIGHT UPON IT.

—*Chief Joseph (Nez Perce), 1879*

the great rock

(OMAHA)

Long ago, at the beginning of it all, everything was in the mind of Wakonda, the Great Spirit. Back then, all things were in the form of spirit. Those spirit beings moved about in the space between the Earth and the stars. They sought somewhere where they could find shape and form. They went to the Sun, but its heat was too great. They went to the moon, but it was too cold. Then they came down to Earth.

Earth was covered with water then. The spirit beings went to the north, to the east, to the south, to the west, but found no place to stand. Then, out of the ancient waters, a Great Rock rose up. Flames came from the Great Rock and clouds formed above the water. Land formed about the Great Rock. Grasses and trees grew upon *that land. Then those spirit beings came down upon the new Earth. They took the shapes of the animals and birds and all things which fly and walk and crawl. The land was filled with their songs of thanks to Wakonda, the Great Spirit, the Maker of All.*

how the earth was made

(SENECA)

Beyond the dome of the sky there is another world. In the most ancient of times, that world was there, a beautiful place. That world floated above this world like a great cloud. In that beautiful place lived the Chief of the Sky World and his people. In the center of that world was a great tree with four white roots that stretched to each of the directions. Flowers and fruits grew on that tree and at its very top was a great white flower that gave light to the Sky World and perfumed the air with its sweet scent. From its base grew leaves of tobacco, whose odor was greatly pleasing to the Ancient Chief.

Then a dream changed everything. Some say that it was the Ancient Chief who dreamed. Some say that the dream came to his young wife, Iagentci, who was expecting a child. That dream commanded the Chief to have the Sky Tree uprooted. When it was done, there was a great hole in the Sky Land. Iagentci came close to look through that hole in the Sky Land and see what was beneath. Then something happened. Some say that Iagentci lost her footing. Some say that she was pushed by the Ancient Chief. All agree that she fell through the hole in the Sky Land and that as she fell, she grasped at the earth of the Sky Land, gathering into her one hand all kinds of seeds that had been shaken from the Sky Tree as it was uprooted. And with her other hand she grasped at the leaves of the tobacco plant. So it was that she took those leaves and those seeds with her as she fell.

The water creatures who lived below looked up and saw Iagentci falling toward the place where they lived. Those water creatures knew that this new one could not live as they did in the water. They quickly held a council and it was agreed that the birds—ducks and geese and swans—would fly up and catch her between their interknit wings. Great Turtle would rise up from the underworld and offer his back as a resting place. This was done and Iagentci was brought down safely to rest on the back of the Great Turtle.

Meanwhile, to make a world for the new one to dwell upon, the water creatures began to dive down to bring up some earth. The duck dove as deeply as he could, but went so deep that he breathed in water and floated up dead. The pickerel then tried, but it, too, could not reach the bottom and it also floated up dead. Other creatures tried, one after another, but all failed. Finally Muskrat tried and managed to bring up a little earth. Some say it was on Muskrat's nose and that Muskrat wiped the earth off onto Great Turtle's shell. Others say that it was held tightly in Muskrat's paw and the notch on the back of Turtle's shell is where Muskrat scraped that earth off.

Then that earth was spread about. As it was spread it grew larger and larger until it became a whole continent. Then, onto that new earth Iagentci sprinkled the seeds she brought from the Sky Land, and from that earth the plants and flowers grew. So this world was made.

the emergence of the people

(DINÉ)

At the beginning there was a place called the Black World. In that world the spirit people and the Holy People lived. It was small and much like a floating island in a sea of mist. There were columns of cloud over each of the four corners of that world, cloud columns of white, blue, yellow, and black. Coyote was there and he visited each of those cloud columns.

First Man was formed in the east, where white cloud and black cloud met. With him was formed the white corn. First Woman was formed in the west where yellow cloud and blue cloud came together. With her was formed the yellow corn, the white shell, and turquoise.

Many kinds of Insect Beings lived in that First World. They began to disagree and fight among themselves. Because of that quarreling, all of those who lived in that First World left that place. They rose up, like clouds, to enter the Blue World through an opening to the east. In the Blue World they found Blue Feathered Beings such as Heron and Blue Jay. They found Wolves and Wildcats, Badgers and Foxes and Mountain Lions. Those beings were fighting with one another.

Coyote traveled through that Second World. Everywhere there was suffering and sorrow. So First Man made it possible for all of the Beings to leave. They climbed up into the Yellow World through an opening to the south.

In this Third World there were six sacred mountains. A great river crossed the land from north to south. This was the Female River. Another great river crossed from east to west. This was the Male River. In this world there was no sun. Turquoise Boy and White Shell Woman lived in this world.

One day, Coyote saw something in the water. It was a baby, the child of Teehooltsodii, Water Monster. Coyote picked that baby up and hid it under his robe. Then it began to rain. There was a great flood. The people climbed higher and higher into the mountains. First Man planted first a cedar tree, then a pine tree, then a male reed to try to reach the top of the sky. At last he planted a female reed and it grew tall enough to reach the Fourth World. The people crowded into that reed and climbed up as the floodwaters rose. When they reached the top, they saw Coyote hiding something. It was the child of Water Monster. They made Coyote give the baby back and when he did so, the water began to go down.

our stories remember

Then the people entered the Fourth World, the Glittering World, the Rainbow World. There First Man and First Woman formed the Four Sacred Mountains from the soil brought by First Man from the Third World. It is among those Four Sacred Mountains, in that Glittering World, that the people live to this day.

From Sky Above and Earth Below

Our stories of how things began tell us a great deal. One of the oldest human questions is "How did this world come to be?" It has been said that every culture has its own genesis story. This is especially true when we look at the hundreds of different cultures of Native North America. In fact, among some American Indian nations the story of the Creation might even be told in more than one way. Moreover, with the coming of Europeans, the Judeo-Christian tale of Genesis (as well as the Bible as a whole) was carefully listened to by Native people and, in some cases, absorbed into their oral traditions alongside, but not replacing, their original Creation stories. (Ironically, among the Cherokees, for example, eighteenth century white writers who encountered retold-in-Cherokee versions of such Biblical tales as Jonah and the whale and Samson assumed it meant that the Cherokees were the Lost Tribe of Israel, rather than just very good listeners.) Today, many contemporary American Indians have no problem thinking of themselves as Christian while still accepting the truth of their old traditions. Rather than seeing this as contradictory, they simply see it as respect for the sacred. Admittedly, some might describe this as illogical. However, failing to apply strict logic to sacred knowledge is not necessarily a bad thing. It brings to mind the words spoken by Orulo, an Igulik Inuit storyteller from northeastern Canada, to the Danish anthropologist Knud Rasmussen, as recorded in *Report of the Fifth Thule Expedition* (1930):

origins

Too much thought only leads to trouble. We Eskimos do not concern ourselves with solving all riddles. We repeat the old stories in the way they were told to us, and with the words we ourselves remember. And if there should then seem to be a lack of reason in the story as a whole, there is yet enough remaining in the way of incomprehensible happenings, which our thought cannot grasp. If it were but everyday ordinary things there would be nothing to believe in.

Some years ago, Jack Gladstone, a Blackfeet Indian friend of mine who is a folk singer, called to tell me a story. He had just checked into a motel room somewhere in the Midwest. When he turned on the television, it was tuned in to the 700 Club, and there was Pat Robertson holding up a copy of *Keepers of the Earth,* a volume I co-authored. Even though the sound was turned down, there was no doubt about what book it was. The beautiful cover painting, done by the Mohawk artist John Kahionhes Fadden, of Mother Earth holding corn, beans, and squash lovingly cradled in her hands was being shot in close-up by the camera. My friend couldn't believe it. Pat Robertson, a Christian evangelist, seemed to be recommending an Indian book. He was right not to believe it. When he turned up the sound, he heard Pat Robertson saying ". . .and this is a bad book that should not be in your schools because it teaches people to worship Mother Earth instead of God." At that point, Jack walked over to the television, put his hands on top of it, and said, "Pat, be healed. It is a metaphor."

Discussing the relative merits of one culture's sacred traditions in comparison to another's is the sort of slippery slope that leads to religious wars. Let me simply say that the frequent acceptance and tolerance of other cultures' sacred stories indicates two things about American Indian cultures. The first is that respect for stories as a whole is deep and widespread. The second is that Native Americans have a healthy respect for and understanding of both symbol and metaphor.

Folklorists speak of certain broad motifs that are found in the Creation stories of the Native peoples of North America. The majority of American Indian nations seem to have some version of one or the other of these as their explanation of how this present world came to be here. Those motifs, such as the Great Rock, the Earthdiver and the Emergence, are quite different from the Judeo-Christian Genesis story. Although it can rightly be said that both the Earthdiver and the story of Noah's Ark in the Old Testament tell of a great flood, the bringing of life to the new Earth could not be more different between the two. There is no sign of any European influence. Thus, we might conclude that they tell us a great deal about the symbolic ways American Indian people see this world.

The Omahas, the Lakotas, and other Plains peoples tell one version or another of the Great Flaming Rock tradition. I find it particularly interesting when we consider the fact that modern science talks of the importance of vulcanism, of the rising of molten lava from the volcanoes of the ancient Earth, as the source of life. Even today, in the islands of Hawaii, we see that powerful primeval force at work, lava flowing into the ocean and making new land before our eyes. Stories like this are one reason why a number of contemporary American Indian thinkers, such as Vine Deloria, Jr., talk about our traditional tales as a sort of "Indian science."

The Seneca tradition is characteristic of the many flood stories told in North America. In this Earthdiver tale one creature or a group of creatures dive down beneath the primeval waters to bring up earth. They then place it on the back of a great turtle, which volunteers to always bear the great burden of the world. One form or another of the Earthdiver Creation story can be found throughout the North American continent—from the Northeast to the California coast. It is so widespread that the image of North America as Turtle Island, the land on the back of Great Turtle, is now a universally understood, Pan-Indian concept.

The current Pan-Indian image of Turtle Island, is, of course, like many of the other aspects of Indian America, partially an outgrowth of intertribalism. The present-day widespread connection between Native tribal nations all across the continent was, as I indicated earlier, unintentionally fostered by government boarding schools, where the children of many American Indian tribal nations came to know one another. But Earthdiver stories were certainly told in virtually every corner of the continent for many generations before Columbus.

Certain shared Pan-Indian images, like Turtle Island, are also a result of the use by American Indians of such means of mass communication as newspapers, through a highly active Native press movement that gained tremendous strength in the second half of the twentieth century. The Native American Journalists Association (NAJA) and such bi-weekly or weekly newspapers as *News from Indian Country* (from Hayward, Wisconsin) and *Indian Country News* (originally from South Dakota and now from Oneida, New York) are the Native equivalents of *USA Today* and *The New York Times*. However, it can certainly also be said that in pre-Columbian America, Native people from tribal nations as far removed from one another as the Iroquois and the California nations, would have recognized the Great Turtle concept. Even in Central America, earthquakes were explained by the Mayans as the result of the Great Turtle shifting about beneath the surface.

Great Turtle, a sentient and ancient reptile, chooses to help all other life. A whole cast of non-human beings plays supporting roles, including the Earthdiver itself. In every version of the Earthdiver story, it is never a human being who dives down to bring up the earth. Loon, Muskrat, Pike, Beaver, Duck—any creature with the powerful ability to move between the world of water and the world of air plays that role. This is emphatically not the Judeo-Christian Creation story. Instead of a human-centered cosmos, we find ourselves in a universe surrounded by sentience and awareness, by non-human beings or beings who combine both animal nature and human qualities. They offer assistance because assistance is needed, because it is the right thing to do. Someone is in need of help. Without question, the water beings hasten to the aid of Sky Woman, even though she is a stranger. They risk their own lives in doing so, and in many versions of the story they actually die trying. (This willingness of other beings— both animal and plant—to consciously choose to assist human life by allowing themselves to be hunted, killed, used for food and clothing and the making of useful objects, continues in the new world.)

Another significant aspect of the Earthdiver story is the relationship between the Sky Land and this Earth. The beings of the Sky Land are neither omniscient nor perfect. They are seen as human-like beings, ruled by an Ancient Chief. All good comes to them from a great Sky Tree. But when a dream is sent to them, they sacrifice that Sky Tree, creating an opening through which life can fall down to this Earth. Where does that dream come from?

I have been told by Native elders from many different nations that their traditions hold that our dreams are messages from the ultimate Creator, the one called the Great Mystery. The importance of listening to one's dreams, properly interpreting them, and then acting upon them in the waking world seems to have been as much a part of American Indian life as it has been in other cultures around the world. However, unlike European thought, where reality and dream are not the same, dreaming is often regarded as very real by Indians. Dreams are sacred. This, by the way, is far from being limited to the past. To this day, it seems that to say, "I have had a dream," takes on a far greater meaning among Indians. I've had plenty of experience with dreams as messages myself—at times in ways I really cannot discuss. Here is one small example that I feel I can share. In 1992, my younger son and I spent time in the Lacandon Mayan village of Naha in the Chiapas region of Mexico. Each morning, Chan K'in, the leader of the village, who was well over one hundred years old, would ask me about my dreams. He would then interpret their meanings in terms of things that were coming to me in ways that often proved surprisingly true.

John Mohawk, a Seneca historian and philosopher, is one of the most brilliant people I have ever known. He has often contrasted European culture with such Native cultures of northeastern North America as the Iroquois in a way that I find both thought-provoking and related to the Earthdiver tradition. European cultures, he explains, are male-dominated. American Indian cultures are woman-centered.

origins

In Judeo-Christian as well as Islamic culture, man is made from the earth and then woman is shaped from one of his ribs. Then man is given control of the Earth, rulership over all living things. In this world, man is made in the image of God. It is not that way among American Indians. Human beings are not seen as the acme of Creation. Instead, they are often described as the weakest of all, the most flawed, and the most forgetful. Further, people are not made in the image of God. God is, in Abenaki, Ktsi Nwaskw, "the Great Mystery." In Mohawk, God is Sonkweadaiso, "the One Who Shapes Us"; in Lakota, Wakan Tanka, "the Great Spirit." And so it goes in many other Native languages. In some way, the shaping and the mysterious nature of the Creator is expressed. "We may see the Creator," my Mohawk friend Tom Porter said, "in a bird or some small thing that comes to us, but no one can look upon the Creator directly. If you did so, you would be destroyed. No one knows what the Creator looks like."

One image, though, that is seen again and again in our Creation stories is that birth comes from women. Although there are stories in which men and women are shaped or appear at the same time, the reversal of nature that occurs when Eve comes out of the body of a man never happens in American Indian traditions. Indeed, when this world on Turtle's back is dreamed into being, the one who brings life from the Sky Land is a woman. The first human-like being to walk upon the Earth is a woman. Further, like that new Earth pregnant with promise, she is expecting a child. That child also turns out to be a girl.

The full telling of the Sky Woman tradition is much longer than the part of the story with which this chapter was begun. Here is a summary of its more important parts: Sky Woman's daughter grows quickly to womanhood. Sky Woman cautions her not to go toward the west. When her mother is away, the child goes to the west, where she meets a man (sometimes in the form of an invisible being who is the West Wind). The daughter becomes pregnant herself with twin boys. One twin is good-minded, but the other, called Flint in the Mohawk version, has a twisted mind. Good Mind is born in the normal fashion, but Flint thrusts himself out through his mother's side, killing her. Flint then tells Sky Woman that Good Mind caused their mother's death. Sky Woman's daughter is buried in the Earth. From her body grow corn, beans, squash, and tobacco. Good Mind and Flint then begin a contest. Good Mind makes things that are useful and beautiful. Flint makes things that are ugly and dangerous. Finally the two engage in a great battle and Flint is cast from this world down into an underworld.

I've been told by Iroquois elders such as Dewasentah, who was the Clan Mother of the Eel Clan at Onondaga, that although Flint is physically gone from our world, his bad thoughts still can influence our minds. So it is important for us to examine our thoughts from time to time to see if we are thinking with the Good Mind or in an angry and twisted way. That idea of anger twisting the mind seems to be very widespread. In fact, in the Plains sign language that was used by more than thirty different Indian nations, the sign for anger is made by pointing at your head and rotating your finger to indicate the confusion and twisting of thought produced by rage.

The story told by the Diné (Navajos) is only one example of that common motif in American Indian Creation stories, the Emergence. Versions of this story are especially prevalent among the southwestern peoples, including the Apaches and the Pueblos. The journey up from the darkness into this world of light and rainbows has been described by some as a gestation myth in which the people emerge from the womb of Mother Earth, climbing up the birth canal. The kivas of the Pueblos, ceremonial structures used only by initiated men, are entered and exited by a ladder in a way that reenacts the emergence from the underworld and a ceremonial rebirth. Within each kiva there is a *sipapu,* a hole in the floor that represents that original place of emergence.

The Diné Emergence story included at the start of this chapter is based on oral tellings I have heard and on the form of the Creation story published by Rough Rock Press (Navajo Curriculum Center) in *Navajo History.* There are many versions of this story in print. Although some of the published versions may differ because they have been misinterpreted or broadly retold by non-Navajos, even traditional Navajo tellers have disagreed about the number of worlds, the events that took place in each, and the colors assigned to each of those worlds. However, all of the Navajo versions agree on the most important aspects of the story.

Once again, as in the story of the Earthdiver, other beings take part in the journey to a new world. They are the Holy People, beings who exist before the creation of actual humans. Rather than falling from the sky, life emerges from beneath the Earth. Again, though, there is a succession of worlds. Further, the emergence is possible only through cooperation, and there is no statement or even implication that mastery over this new world is given to human beings. One of the most important aspects of each of the successive worlds is balance. When there is balance, all is well. But when the balance is upset—as in the case of Coyote taking the water baby—there are terrible consequences. The role of Coyote, as Trickster and even Creator, will be discussed in a later chapter. But for now it is enough to note that he certainly serves as a good example of bad behavior.

Later on, those same Holy People, who include Coyote, First Man and First Woman, and numerous others, will become the pantheon of powerful beings to whom human beings may turn when they are seeking to be healed. The lessons of balance in the Emergence story are carried over into everyday life. Sickness is seen as a result of the loss of balance, while health is the desired and normal state. The possibility of disorder and the threat of danger may be all around us in this world (as they were in the worlds before this one), but if we proceed through life with care and control, our paths will be good and it will bring us blessings.

When we look at both of these American Indian traditions—that of the Earthdiver story and that of the Emergence—we see that they have some very important things in common, things that reflect and continue to influence the way Native people see themselves in the world. We live in a world where all things are related to one another. In this world, where cooperation made everything

our stories remember

possible and unselfish sacrifice unleashed the power of creation, humans are no more important than animals or plants. To maintain this world we must strive for physical and spiritual equilibrium. Anger, imbalance, and self-centered actions or thoughts may cause hardship. Health and all desirable things may come as a result of generosity and good thought.

Recommended Reading

Momaday, N. Scott (Kiowa). *The Way to Rainy Mountain.* Albuquerque: University of New Mexico Press, 1969. Momaday won the Pulitzer Prize in 1969 for his novel *House Made of Dawn.* Many feel that this short nonfiction book, which blends Kiowa oral traditions and more contemporary tales with Momaday's own reflective essays, is a masterwork that marks the true beginning of the American Indian literary renaissance.

Penn, W. S. (Nez Perce/Osage). *The Telling of the World: Native American Stories and Art.* New York: Stewart, Tabori & Chang, 1996. "Stories," Penn says in his introduction, "make our world." Beautifully illustrated, this wide-ranging volume of legends and stories from many tribes follows the path of life.

indians and art

Our Mother the Earth, Our Father the Sky,
Weave for us a garment of brightness;
Let the warp be the white morning light,
Let the weft be the red evening light,
Let the fringes be the falling rain,
Let the border be the standing rainbow;
Weave for us a garment of brightness,
That we may walk in the right way where birds sing…

—from a Tewa song

Long ago, Corn Husk Doll had the most beautiful face. Corn Husk Doll knew this better than anyone. She would stare at her own face for hours in the calm water of the lake. She boasted about her beauty. One day, as she was admiring herself, the wind rippled the water. Her reflection disappeared. Corn Husk Doll touched her face with her hands. Her face was gone. Ever since then, all corn husk dolls are made without a face. This reminds people not to be too vain.

Just as making corn husk dolls is an example of the way traditional American Indian art connects with the cycles of the natural world, so the story of Corn Husk Doll losing her face illustrates yet again how our stories are used to both educate and amuse. Although a great deal of contemporary American Indian art—sculptures, textiles, paintings, even videos—may seem to be nothing more than decorative or "art for art's sake," with a closer look you may discover that art is still connected to its ancient roots and that it still contains a lesson. It remembers that all things are connected and that humans must always acknowledge those connections.

In northern New Mexico a Cochiti Pueblo girl and her mother stand by a pit below a tall mesa. They are about to gather clay for the making of pots. Before they do so, the mother thanks the spirit of the clay, promising that they will be careful and respectful with whatever they gather from the pit. The little girl listens closely, learning from her mother's words. Later that day, she both watches and helps as they pick small sticks and stones from the dry clay and then place it in a bucket to soak up water. The long, careful process of preparing the clay will take many days, but it will be worth it. Together they will make pots that are beautiful and useful.

Native American art has always been about respect and beauty. We must be thankful for what we receive from Mother Earth. Such gifts from earth and plants and animals as clay and wood and leather make it possible for us to survive. For thousands of years, Native people have made things that are both useful and attractive, learning to do so by the time-honored process of helping and watching their elders.

In the past, Native American art was directly connected to the ecosystems of the different parts of the North American continent. Today, even when they use electric tools to carve wood and stone, weave on a modern loom, or paint on a canvas, contemporary American Indian artists still remember and refer to nature.

Because of its unique beauty, Native American art is displayed in museums around the world. Designs drawn from different Native peoples appear on T-shirts and corporate logos. Work created thousands of years ago and new pieces by Indian artists are treasured. However, many people do not realize the deeper meaning of Native American art. American Indian art reflects Native culture, tells us stories, and helps us see how we are connected to nature and to each other.

indians and art

Wherever American Indian people lived, their cultures and their art were very connected to the ecology of their place. The Pacific Northwest has the ocean, a great deal of rain, and large, tall trees. Thus objects made of redwood and cedar and symbols connected to the sea are very important to such American Indian nations as the Kwakiutls, the Haidas, the Makahs, and others who carved wood and hunted and fished in the ocean. Their homes were big houses made of planks that were cut from the living trees. The majority of the traditional stories and symbols of the Northwest are about the ocean. On the Great Plains, where there was little water and great herds of animals, an entirely different way of life evolved in which hunting was central. The homes of such Plains Indians as the Cheyennes, the Kiowas, the Lakotas, and the Crows were conical tipis covered with the skin of the buffalo.

Just as all things in the natural world are connected, so, too, is the sacred connected to everyday life. Some kinds of American Indian art are very deeply connected to traditional religious practices. In the words of art historian Arthur Silberman, in *100 Years of Native American Painting* (a catalog for a 1978 exhibit at the Oklahoma Museum of Art), until approximately 1880, "Native American painting was a form of religious expression and a kind of shorthand used mainly to record personal and tribal histories."

Traditional sacred art has sometimes been popularized and sold by Native people themselves. In the Southwest, Pueblo kachina dolls and Navajo (Diné) sand paintings are two prominent examples. Kachinas are the ancestral and nature spirits who bring the much-needed rain, existing in the form of rain clouds for much of the year. Pueblo men dress in elaborate clothing and masks to represent the spirits of those beings in ceremonial dances held at certain times of the year. Small carved dolls of the various kachinas are used to teach Pueblo children. Such kachina dolls have been openly sold since the early twentieth century. Some Pueblo people say, however, that the only right way to receive a kachina doll is as a gift.

Navajo sand paintings, or dry paintings, are part of healing ceremonies. A Navajo *hataaX̌ii* healer and his assistants make dry paintings by sprinkling different colored sands and powdered bark onto the earth, creating a beautiful and symmetrical picture. Every healing ceremony has its own sand painting. The figures in each picture represent different holy people from sacred stories, such as the Hero Twins who fought dangerous monsters. The person to be healed sits on top of the painting while the ceremony, which includes singing and dancing and the presence of many people showing their support, goes on. When it is over, the colored sands are gathered up and released back into the desert.

Today, modern Diné artists and even American Indians from other tribes make imitation sand paintings by sprinkling colored materials onto a sticky surface. Such paintings, which are designed to be sold to tourists who can hang them on a wall, show how modern artists may use their ancient traditions in new ways. However, a real sand painting is not meant to last.

Iroquois masks are an example of sacred Native art that has not been adapted for commercial purposes. These carved basswood masks, which have been called "false faces," have long been used by teachers to discuss Iroquois culture. Throughout much of the late nineteenth and twentieth centuries, such masks were displayed in museums all over the world.

Today, the most influential Iroquois traditionalists have stated publicly that it is wrong to sell or display these masks. These creations are not just objects of wood, but living things, sacred beings who wish themselves to be seen only at certain times of the year and in certain ceremonies, kept hidden away from sight until such times arrive. Even a photograph or a drawing of such a mask is now regarded as unacceptable. In fact, because of the strong objections of the Iroquois, museums all over the United

indians and art

States and Canada have removed "false face" masks from their collections and repatriated them, giving them back to the Iroquois. (Other tribal nations, especially the Native peoples of the far Northwest and Alaska, have different traditions about their own masks. Masks of the Yupiks of Alaska, for example, are still widely displayed and sold, and there has been either very little or no objection to this by tradition-bearers.)

One form of traditional Iroquois art that is now widely shared by the Iroquois with non-Indians is the corn husk doll, whose story appears above. In late summer, when the first corn is ripe, the Iroquois have a Green Corn Festival to give thanks for that harvest. From the husks of the ears of corn, corn husk dolls are still crafted by both children and adults. (Instructions on how to make a Corn Husk doll can be found in the book *Native American Gardening*, by Michael Caduto and Joseph Bruchac.) Today, such dolls are made by some Iroquois artists and dressed in buckskin clothing decorated with beads. The dolls are sold not just as toys for children, but as works of art. But, whether she is a simple toy for a child or an elaborately decorated collector's item, Corn Husk Doll, like all American Indian art, still carries her ancient story.

spirit: life and death

WE ARE THE STARS WHO SING,

WHO SING WITH THEIR LIGHT.

WE ARE THE BIRDS OF FIRE,

WHO FLY OVER THE SKY.

OUR LIGHT IS A VOICE,

WITH OUR SONG WE MAKE A ROAD,

A ROAD FOR THE SPIRIT TO CROSS OVER.

—translated circa 1897

from an ancient Passamaquoddy song

spirit: life and death

the coming of death

(WESTERN SHOSHONE)

Long ago, Gray Wolf and Coyote were out walking around. It was before anyone had died. But they knew that one day death would enter the world. They came to the Salmon River.

"Urrh. How shall we decide about the way death will be?" Gray Wolf said.

"Let us, uh, do it this way-pai," said Coyote. "You, uh, speak first about death, eh? But I, uh, yes, I will speak last-pai."

Gray Wolf picked up a piece of wood.

"Urrh. I think it should be this way when people die," Gray Wolf said. "I will throw this wood into the water. If the wood floats, then people will die, but after four days have passed, they will come back to life again."

Then Gray Wolf threw the piece of wood into the water, and it floated. "A-hi-e!" Gray Wolf said. He was pleased. But Coyote had not yet spoken. It was now Coyote's turn.

Coyote picked up a stone. "I, uh, think it should be this-a way-pai," Coyote said. "I, uh, will throw this-a, er, uh, into the water-pai. If it floats, yes, then it will be as you said-pai. But if, uh, er, it sinks, eh? Then people will, uh, die and not, no, not come back to this world again-pai."

Then Coyote threw the stone into the water. It sank, and so, because Coyote spoke last, that was the way death came into this world. People died and they did not come back to life.

"This, uh, is how it should be-pai," Coyote said. "If, er, uh, everyone just kept on living, the world would, uh, be too crowded-pai."

One day, though, Coyote's wife died. On that day he changed his mind about death. He decided it was better that people not stay dead forever. So he went to the place where the spirits of those who have died stay. It was a long journey. When he got there those who had died greeted him. His wife was glad to see him.

"Coyote! I thought you would never come here," she said to her husband.

"I, uh, am only, uh, visiting-pai," Coyote said.

Then he put his wife's spirit into a basket and started carrying her back to this world. If he could get all the way back without opening the basket, she would be able to come back to life. It went well for a few days, but it was a long journey. Coyote began to wonder how his wife's spirit was doing.

"It, er, uh, would not hurt to take a look, eh? I will, uh, see if she is well-pai," he said to himself. Then he opened the basket just a crack. But that was enough. As soon as he opened it, the basket was empty. Coyote's wife was gone. And ever since then, no one has ever come back to this world after they have died.

I had thought of making this the final chapter in this book. Then I realized that I was thinking about things in a European way, where there is a linear progression beginning with life and ending with death. Straight-line thinking is as characteristic of European cultures as is the concept of the human world as a pyramid. Hierarchy was long seen as the normal and natural way, a way ordained by God himself. Picture that societal pyramid as a series of levels. At the top, all alone in his god-like glory and power was the king. Just below him were the dukes and barons and the other noble lords who ruled their fiefdoms just as the king did his country. The next level was the clergy, who often were nearly as powerful and wealthy as the nobles themselves. In fact, because of the laws of primogeniture, which meant only the eldest son could inherit the father's wealth, many of the sons of the nobility entered the clergy. Like the noble class, the clergy were often landowners in their own right. Farther down were the merchants, the growing middle class who had some wealth and some property, but nothing like those above them. The last level, the most numerous of all, those who were bearing the weight of all those above, were the serfs. They worked the land but seldom owned it. Their lives were short and their opportunities limited to the trades of the working class. There was no upward mobility. One's fate was predestined from the cradle to the grave. From the British Isles to the steppes of Russia, from the North Sea to the Mediterranean, this was the Europe of the sixteenth, seventeenth and eighteenth centuries. There was no such thing as real democracy, despite the roots of that word in an ancient Greek city-state (where every free man had an equal vote, but there were no voting rights for slaves or women).

The American Indian vision of life and death, of human societies, of the place of the individual in the world, was neither the straight line nor the pyramid. Instead, as I explain in the introduction, it was the circle. In life, the idea of the circle meant that there was, indeed, inherent equality or at least equal opportunity to gain status and respect within your individual tribal culture. Although the roles of men and women differed, as I discuss in a later chapter, women played roles that were acknowledged to be at least as important as those of men. In some tribal cultures the women played a major part in choosing leaders. There were situations in which even a person from another tribal nation (or, in fact, a European) could be fully adopted and gain all the rights of a person born into that nation—to the point of becoming a tribal leader.

The greatest of all circles was that of life and death. Ideas of an afterlife, or reincarnation, vary greatly among the many different cultures of North America, but the sense of a circle can be found in all of them, even if it was simply the certainty that after death our bodies would re-enter the great circle of life itself. Our flesh would feed the animals and plants just as those animals and plants fed us. Our lives would be reborn in the song and flow of vital energy that is always all around us. Though changed, our spirits would not be lost.

The Road of Stars

Today, the lights of our cities make it hard for many to see the heavens. However, if you can find some place where carbon arc lamps have not blurred those bright distant lights of the night, you may see that great sweep of stars that has touched the minds and spirits of human beings from time immemorial. The Chinese named it the River of Heaven. To modern astronomers and much of the Western world it is known as the Milky Way, the galaxy of which our sun and the solar system are part. But to many of the American Indian nations of North America, those innumerable stars are seen as a sky road, a path traveled by the souls of the dead, an eternal trail where each star marks the footstep or the spirit of one who left this life.

In her 1997 book *Stars of the First People: Native American Star Myths and Constellations,* Dorcas S. Miller lists more than fifty of the names given to the Milky Way by different tribal nations. Nearly all of those names envision it as some sort of road or trail, and each name has its own story. Although not all of them describe this sky trail as the path taken by our spirits, the large number of those that do and the geographical range of those nations show how widespread this belief has been throughout the continent. In the Southeast, the Muskogee Creeks named it Spirits' Road. To the Pawnees, Omahas, and Lakotas of the Great Plains it is Spirits' Path. The Southern Paiutes of the Great Basin region call it Sky Path, while the Shoshones refer to it as People's Trail. To the Crees, Montagnais, and Naskapis of the Subarctic it is Ghost Road.

A careful study of Miller's list suggests, however, that it is in the eastern woodlands, among Iroquoian and Algonquin peoples, where the Milky Way as the path followed by human souls is the most commonly accepted vision. From my own experience of hearing such traditions for more than forty years, this certainly seems to be true. Moreover, those stories are emphatically not just a part of our past, but deeply connected to the present-day experiences of contemporary American Indians, including members of my own family. Our tales of the Sky Trail tell us a great deal about the enduring strength and sustaining spirit that come from our traditions. Further, not only people, but also animals (in sometimes surprising ways), are associated with that journey to the afterworld, reminding us of the intimate and mysterious connections among all living things.

The Iroquois say that the Milky Way's innumerable stars mark the footprints of the dead who have traveled that blessed path. Because the Iroquois use the first strawberries that appear each spring to make a sacred medicinal drink, it should be no surprise to hear that wild strawberries grow along the edges of that heavenly road. In fact, as the Seneca Indian folklorist Arthur C. Parker attested in *The Code of Handsome Lake* in 1912, Iroquois people recovering from serious illnesses often say, "I almost ate strawberries." (Those same words were spoken to me only a few years ago by a Mohawk friend who had to undergo bypass surgery.) Handsome Lake was the Seneca prophet whose great vision after a near-death experience at the turn of the nineteenth century led to a rebirth of Iroquois traditional practices. Here, in a passage from his Gaiwiio, or "Good Message," as translated by Parker, Handsome Lake speaks of the Sky Trail that was shown him by four sacred messengers while he was "dead":

> Then they went upon the narrow road and had not gone far along it when a far more brilliant light appeared. It was then that they smelled the fragrant odors of the flowers along the road. Delicious looking fruits were growing on the wayside and every kind of bird flew in the air above them. The most marvelous and beautiful things were on every hand. And all these things were on the heaven road.

In 1609 the Virginia Company chose Sir Samuel Argall to be the "pilot of Virginia," succeeding Captain Christopher Newport, who had brought the first English colonists to Jamestown. In William Strachey's *The History of Travel into Virginia Brittanica,* finished in 1612 but not published until 1758, the following incident concerning Argall's visit to "the Indians of the Patawameck River, the last year, 1610, about Christmas" is described. Iopassus, the *werowance* (or chief) of the town of Matchipongo came on board Argall's ship. He brought with him a fifteen-year-old boy named Henry Spellman. In an unusual cultural exchange, Spellman had been "sold" by Captain John Smith to the Powhatan Indians to learn their language and act as an interpreter between the two peoples. After more than a year of living among the Native peoples of Virginia, Spellman was fluent in the language and, it seemed, healthier, better fed, and happier than the English in Jamestown, where more than half the colonists died from such things as starvation and the "bloody flux" from drinking the polluted river water during the first eighteen months of the colony. Spellman was asked to interpret the biblical story of the Creation of the world to Iopassus. Iopassus listened well, but then "bade the boy to tell the captain, if he would hear, he would tell him the manner of **their** beginning...." Spellman's recounting of the Powhatan Creation tale, in which Great Hare makes the people, led Argall to ask "what he thought became of them after death." This was his answer:

> ...after they are dead here they go to the top of a high tree; and there espy a fair plain, a broad pathway, on both sides whereof doth grow all manner of pleasant fruits as mulberries, strawberries, plums, etc. In this pleasant path they run toward the rising of the sun, where the godlike Hare's house is...where they find their forefathers living in great pleasure in a goodly field, where they do nothing but dance and sing and feed on delicious fruits with that Great Hare, who is their great god. And when they have lived there until they become stark old men, they say they die there likewise by turns and come into the world again.

Although Iopassus does not mention that this is the Road of Stars, by comparing it with the passage from the Good Message and by connecting it to the traditions of the neighboring Algonquin peoples—whose languages and cultures were nearly identical—only a hundred miles to their north, it seems clear what trail it is that the spirits of those who have died are now walking.

Spirit: life and death

The Lenape people, whose traditional homeland stretches from what is now Pennsylvania and New Jersey up along the lower Hudson River, also describe the Milky Way as the road to the afterworld. They say that there is a bridge along the Star Road at the place where the Milky Way appears to fork. That bridge is guarded by the dogs that each person owned while they were alive on Earth. If you were kind to your dogs and treated them well, they will be waiting for you and will help you to cross safely. If you mistreated your dogs, they will block your path.

While the stars are the footprints of the spirits to some Native peoples, to others those bright lights are the spirits themselves. Gladys Tantaquidgeon is a Mohegan elder, anthropologist, and medicine woman who celebrated her 101st birthday in 2000. She speaks of that "ultimate trek" as the Beautiful White Path. In *Medicine Trail,* a 2000 biography about Gladys written by her niece Melissa Fawcett (Tantaquidgeon), it is noted that "Stars are the advanced form taken by Indian people with extraordinary gifts of the spirit after they pass into the spirit world." The Milky Way itself is, to the Mohegans, the Smoky Way, so called because ceremonial pipe smoke "follows that Beautiful Path as it enters the blackness of the cosmos" carrying our prayers to the great celestial beings.

It is commonly said among Native peoples that when a person dies, his or her spirit takes the shape of a light while the person's body returns to again become part of the earth. That light must then journey to a high point, which might be a mountain, a hill, or even the tallest tree. For my own Abenaki people, that spot is Wonbi Wadzoak, the White Mountain. It may not be one particular mountain for every Abenaki group, since I have heard it variously identified as Mount Washington in New Hampshire, Camel's Hump in Vermont, and Katahdin in Maine, but simply the highest point of land that can serve as a stepping-stone to the start of the Sky Trail.

Sometimes, though, those spirit lights become lost and cannot find their way to that first step. Here are two more stories, both of them from the present day, that speak about finding the way to the Sky Trail.

The first of them was told to me three years ago by an Onondaga friend of mine, Mike Tarbell. Mike had been doing a workshop on Iroquois hunting traditions at the Iroquois Indian Museum in Howe's Cave, New York. After talking about the deep respect and love that Iroquois people have for the deer— whose meat and skins and bones sustained his people in the way the buffalo did the Plains nations—Mike went on to say that the deer have been given a special job to help guide our spirits. "Sometimes," he said, "a person's spirit becomes lost when it is seeking the Sky Road. You might see that spirit light wandering confused through the forest. When the deer see one of those spirit lights, they run at it and catch it in their horns and then throw it up into the sky, above the trees, to start it on its journey." Then Mike shook his head sadly. "Maybe that is why so many deer get hit at night by cars. They see those headlights and run toward them. They think that they are a lost spirit trying to find its way."

There were tears in my eyes as I listened to Mike tell that story, not just for the sacrifice of the deer, but also because it connected so deeply to a family story that I didn't hear until I was in my fifties. Because there was so much shame connected to being Indian, there was little talk about our Abenaki heritage when I was young. But one late-spring day we were able to bring my mother and her four elderly cousins— Howard, Lillian, John, and Edith Bowman—together at our home in Greenfield Center. At some point, Lillian, the oldest of them, began to talk about her grandfather Lewis Bowman. Lewis had been born in Canada, listing his birthplace as St. Francis, but he came to Troy, New York, and enlisted in the United States Army to serve in the Civil War. Grievously wounded and left for dead on March 25, 1865, at the battle of Hatcher's Run, Virginia, he'd survived by drinking the water that puddled around him as a thunderstorm swept over the field, and he lived to father thirteen children.

"Grampa Lewis's favorite," Lillian said, "was his little grandson Ed. He called him 'my little Eddie.' When Grampa Lewis was dying, back in 1918, it was early autumn and there was an influenza epidemic. Eddie was six then. Grampa

Spirit: life and death

Lewis's last words were 'How's my little Eddie?' No one had the heart to tell him that Eddie had just died of influenza that same afternoon. Later that night, we all saw it." Lillian paused and looked at her hands folded in her lap. "We saw a little light out there, wandering around in the field like it was lost. Then a bigger light came back down the hill. That little light went right up to it and bounced around it. Then the two of them, the big light and the little one, they went up the hill together and disappeared into the stars. We all knew those two lights was Grampa Lewis and his little Eddie."

Whether Star Road, or Great Sky Road, Last Trail to the Happy Home, Soul's Road, or Spirit Path, our traditions about that last (perhaps) journey along the ancient road of souls teach us many things. They show not only our attitudes toward death and dying, but also the ancient and sacred understanding that dying is not a final act, but a link between worlds, part of a great eternal circle.

Recommended Reading

Beck, Peggy; Walters, Anna Lee (Pawnee/Otoe); and Francisco, Nia (Navajo). *The Sacred: Ways of Knowledge, Sources of Life.* Tsaile, Ariz.: Navajo Community College Press, 1977. This is an uncommonly wide-ranging exploration of the way American Indians traditionally see and experience the sacred. No other book does a better job of examining the common ground of our sacred traditions.

reservations

They are taking us beyond Miami
They are taking us beyond the Caloosa River
They are taking us to the end of our tribe…
They are taking us to an old town in the west

—*from a Seminole song*

As more and more white settlers arrived in North America, American Indians found themselves dispossessed of their land. Through treaties, land sales (frequently coerced), and military action, the Native people were forced from their homes. The practice of relocating and concentrating Indian populations on tracts of land whose boundaries were set by the dominant culture became accelerated in the nineteenth century. Tracts of land that were not relinquished, but were reserved for Indians, became known as reservations. Although these areas were supposed to be for the use of the Indian nation alone, in perpetuity, many American Indian nations found themselves forced to move again and again, as lands farther to the west were designated as "Indian Territory."

The first Indian reservation in what would be the United States was created by the Puritans in 1639 for the Quinnipiacs of Connecticut. Its existence was short-lived. As was the case in a great number of the original reservation lands east of the Mississippi, the concentration of Indians into small areas of their original lands was only the first step to Indian Removal. The Quinnipiacs (like many other Connecticut nations) were forced from the state and eventually merged with other tribes. This happened many times with many tribes. The Munsees, a branch of the Mahican Nation of the

Hudson River Valley in New York, were forced east to Massachusetts, where they became known as the Stockbridge Indians. From Massachusetts, they were then sent west again. Eventually, they ended up in Wisconsin, where they are known as the Stockbridge Munsees. In some cases, the land that was supposed to be reserved for Native people was taken from them before they ever received it. Few know that the exact area of Washington, D.C., was designated to be set aside as a reservation for the Indians of the Maryland tidewater region before it was chosen to be the site of the American nation's capital.

The purpose of the policy of Indian reservations and Indian Removal was sometimes described as benevolent. Thomas Jefferson felt that the creation of Indian Territory to the west of the Mississippi River would protect the innocent Indians from being taken advantage of by predatory whites. (Of course, it also freed up Indian land, such as that in Georgia, where the discovery of gold in Cherokee territory was a major factor leading to the Trail of Tears.) There, they would be safe for many generations. Untroubled by corrupt whites, and guided toward a proper Christian existence by white missionaries, they would gradually give over their primitive ways and become civilized. Jefferson was wrong—just as he was wrong when he stated that it would take a thousand years for the West to be settled by whites, a process that was accomplished by the end of the nineteenth century.

The best description for many of the nineteenth-century Indian reservations of the West is that they were concentration camps. There the Indians were disarmed, held under the watchful eye of the army, and forbidden to leave, even though the land was usually too poor for either hunting or raising crops. Without the food supplied them by the United States government—which was often late or of very poor quality—the people on most reservations were in frequent danger of starving. When

Indians left their reservations without permission, they were hunted down by the army.

Although dozens of tribes were sent to Indian Territory or forced onto reservation lands much smaller than they had originally been free to use, even those reserved lands were not safe. Traditionally, Indian land is held in common, and the land included in reservations was untaxed. In 1887, the Indian Allotment Act was passed by the federal government. It was designed to end the reservation system by breaking up the commonly held land into individual allotments of 160 acres per person. Many, but not all, reservations were allotted. The Oklahoma land rush was one result of this policy because, after individual allotment to Indians, the remaining land was now in the hands of the government to do with as it wished. Not only did allotment free the bulk of the land for white homesteaders to claim, but it made it impossible for many Indians to afford to keep their own land because they now had to pay taxes and frequently had no money and no way to earn money short of selling their land. In 1907, prior to Oklahoma's statehood, nearly all of the reservations in Oklahoma were dissolved. Only the Omaha Reservation in the northern part of the state survives to this day. Although Oklahoma remains one of the states with the largest proportion of Indians, and its many tribes are still active cultural and political entities, other lands owned by Oklahoma's tribes are Historic Indian Areas, not reservations. The idea of ending all reservations and treaties resurfaced in 1953 with House Concurrent Resolution 108 calling for termination of the federal relationship with tribes. Although there was substantial Indian opposition, from 1955 to 1959 dozens of tribes (including the Menominees of Wisconsin, the Klamaths of Oregon and more than sixty small bands and tribes in western Oregon, the rancherias— Indian tribal communities of California—the Utes and Southern Paiutes of Utah, and the Catawbas of South Carolina) were terminated, with disastrous results. The policy affected 1.3 million acres of tribal lands, and once again, a great deal of that Indian land was lost. Finally, termination itself was terminated in the 1970s, and many of the previously terminated tribes were reinstated.

American Indians are United States citizens, but the official status of each tribe is that of a "nation within a nation." Indian nations have their own governments, laws, and law enforcement agencies. This means that while under federal jurisdiction, Indian reservations are not governed by the laws of the state in which they are located, and Indians on reservations do not have to pay taxes. This special status has made it possible for Indians on some reservations to create economic opportunities by selling certain products tax-free and establishing gaming operations, such as the now-famous Mashuntucket Pequot Foxwoods Casino in Connecticut.

The current American Indian population of the United States is about two million. Of those two million, only about one-third live on reservations, rancherias, or other Indian land. However, the American Indian reservations in the United States have begun to experience a small increase in population as a result of a number of factors. One of the most important is successful Indian claims regarding land taken unfairly in the past through government mismanagement and fraud. There are more than 150 organized, but unrecognized, Indian tribes. Some, like my own Abenaki Nation, never signed treaties with the United States. Others, like the Pequots, survived despite the fact that they were "officially exterminated" during the colonial period. A few of the unrecognized tribes have been able to gain federal recognition in recent years, and in a few notable cases, such as the Pequots and the Mohegans of Connecticut, have used some of the money earned by successful gaming operations to increase their land base. The current American Indian land base in the United States is about fifty-five million acres.

trickster's turn

MANY THINGS ABOUT THE STORY ARE FUNNY, BUT THE STORY IS NOT

FUNNY. IF MY CHILDREN HEAR THE STORIES THEY WILL GROW UP TO

BE GOOD PEOPLE; IF THEY DON'T HEAR THEM, THEY WILL TURN OUT

TO BE BAD. IF COYOTE DID NOT DO ALL THESE THINGS, THEN THOSE

THINGS WOULD NOT BE POSSIBLE IN THE WORLD.

—Yellowman (Diné), 1969

iktomi and the ducks

(LAKOTA)

Iktomi the Trickster was walking along. He had been walking for a long time, and he was feeling hungry. He was so hungry he felt as if he were being cut in half. Then, as he was walking along, he passed by a big lake. Far out in the middle of

that lake he could see many fat ducks. They were too far away for him to reach them, but he had an idea. He quickly gathered some green wood and put it into his bag. Then, bent low with the weight of his bag on his back, he walked along the shore of the lake. The ducks saw him and wondered what he was carrying. They swam closer to ask.

"Iktomi," the ducks called, "what is that on your back?"

But Iktomi acted as if he did not hear them.

"Iktomi," the ducks called again, "what is that on your back?"

Once again, Iktomi continued on his way as if he had heard nothing. Finally, when the ducks asked him the fourth time, he stopped and looked up at them.

"Younger Brothers," he said, "you ask me what I am carrying? I am carrying a bag full of songs. It is so heavy because I have met no one who will dance for me while I sing them. I have met no one who will ask me to sing my new songs."

"Iktomi," said the ducks, "will you sing your new songs for us? We will dance if you sing them."

"Younger Brothers," Iktomi said, "Waste yelo. That is good. I will go make my tipi ready for you.

Then Iktomi went back to his lodge to get ready for the dance. He made a fire in the middle of the floor inside his tipi. But when the fire was burning well, he placed those green sticks on it so that it would be very smoky.

When the ducks came to his lodge, Iktomi invited them in. He held his playing stick in one hand and his drum in the other.

"Hau, kola," Iktomi said. "Hello, my friends. I will tell you the right way to do this. You must all dance in a circle, one after the other. You must sing with me while I sing. But there is much smoke from this fire. As soon as you enter my lodge you must close your eyes and keep them shut or they will get red and sore."

The ducks did just as Iktomi told them to do. They closed their eyes as they came into the lodge so their eyes wouldn't get red. They began to dance around in a circle one after the other while Iktomi played his drum and sang loudly.

But as the ducks danced with their eyes closed, Iktomi put his drum down, even though he kept playing it. Now he had one hand free. He reached out and grabbed a duck when it danced close to him. As Iktomi broke its neck, that duck let out a loud shriek.

"Waste!" Iktomi cried. "That is good. Sing loudly, Little Brother."

Then he grabbed another duck and wrung its neck. He would have gotten all of those ducks if it had not been for the fact that Little Duck noticed that it seemed as if fewer and fewer people were singing now. Little Duck opened her eyes just a little and saw Iktomi's hand reaching out for her.

"Iktomi is killing us, Iktomi is killing us," Little Duck squawked.

All of the ducks that remained flew up in the air and escaped, taking Iktomi's tipi with them. Iktomi was so angry that he kicked at Little Duck as she flew by him. He hit her in the backside so hard that it knocked her legs back on her body. To this day you can see that her legs are farther back than those of any other duck and so she is not a very good dancer. Just as Iktomi said, when she opened her eyes, they got red from the smoke. So it is that she is now called Little Red-eyed Duck, the coot. All coots have red eyes to this day.

Iktomi looked around. Most of the ducks had escaped, but he still had managed to kill a few of them. So he decided to cook them. He got some clay mud and covered each of the ducks with it so they would bake inside that clay. Then Iktomi stuck the clay-covered ducks into the red-hot embers of his fire with only their feet sticking out.

"These ducks will taste good," Iktomi said. "Now I will lie back and rest until they are ready."

However, as soon as Iktomi closed his eyes, he heard a loud, disagreeable squeaking sound.

Wheek-keek, wheek-keek.

It came from overhead.

"Whoever you are, stop that noise. You are bothering me," Iktomi said. But the noise did not stop. It was a tree squeak, the sound of two branches rubbing together in the wind.

trickster's turn

Wheek-keek, wheek-keek.

"Stop that now!"

Wheek-keek, wheek-keek.

"If you don't stop, I will make you stop."

Wheek-keek, wheek-keek.

"All right, I warned you. Now I am going to make you stop," Iktomi said. He climbed high up into the tree, found the two branches that were rubbing together, and pulled them apart. Just as he did so, the wind blew very hard. The branches slipped out of his hands and snapped together around his wrists, trapping him up in the tree. However, even though he was caught, Iktomi was very pleased with himself.

"You see," Iktomi said, "I have made you stop making that noise."

Iktomi looked down. He could see his ducks cooking.

"Ah," Iktomi said. "Soon they will be cooked just right. I hope no one else smells them and comes to eat them while I am stuck up here."

Iktomi looked around and he saw something that worried him. There, far away, a wolf was walking along. "Oh no," Iktomi said. "That wolf might eat my ducks." That wolf had not smelled the ducks cooking and was just walking away.

However, before the wolf disappeared over the hill, Iktomi called out as loudly as he could. "Wolf, Wolf, listen to what I have to say!" Iktomi shouted.

Wolf looked back over his shoulder. "What is it, Iktomi? I am listening."

"Wolf," Iktomi shouted, "do not come over here! If you do, then you will find my ducks cooking and you will eat them."

"Urrh," Wolf said, "indeed I will. Thank you for telling me, Iktomi."

Wolf trotted right over to the fire. He pulled out the ducks and ate them, leaving nothing but their feet. Then Wolf left.

After Wolf had gone, the wind blew again so hard that the branches trapping Iktomi's wrists were blown apart and Iktomi fell out of the tree. He looked at all that was left of his ducks.

"Hunh," Iktomi said, "those ducks were too bony to eat. I did not really want to eat them."

Then Iktomi went on his way.

I did not intend this chapter to be about Trickster. But that is the way it happens with all the American Indian Tricksters, with Iktomi and Coyote, Rabbit and Raven, and all their sisters and brothers. They always show up when you least expect them. And it is right that they should.

One of the things that seems to both fascinate and confuse non-Indians the most is Trickster. Such prominent ethnologists as Paul Radin and Franz Boas have remarked on the inconsistency of having a character who is profoundly sacred and clever on the one hand and incomprehensibly stupid on the other.

(Happy to hear that, Coyote says.)

Okay, okay, but just listen for a minute. How can you have a character such as Coyote who is the Creator of the people one moment and then a total buffoon the next? Not only that, he is dishonest, deceitful, totally libidinous and licentious, as dirty and malodorous as two-day-old road kill. Everything about the American Indian Trickster seems to be the antithesis of the image of the Indian that non-Indians still appear to be most comfortable and most familiar with, the noble nineteenth-century Indian—in particular, the Hiawatha of Henry Wadsworth Longfellow.

The Song of Hiawatha. Throughout much of the twentieth century every high school student in America was introduced to that poem, which still resonates in that part of my own memory shared by such advertising jingles as "Use Ajax, bum bum, the foaming cleanser, baba baba bumbumbum, floats the dirt right down the drain." Doggerel sticks to you like doo-doo does to a shoe.

"By the shores of Gitche-gumee," Longfellow's American epic begins, mixing the conventions of Western poetry (in this case, the trochaic meter of the *Kalevala*, the epic poem of Finland) with Ojibway words and traditions. *Gitche-Gumee,* for example, actually does mean "Great Lake," the original Anishinabe name for Lake Superior. Just as *Nokomis* really does mean "Grandmother." Longfellow's Hiawatha stands tall and strong in all he does, fights the monsters, wins the heart of the fair Minnehaha, and ends his heroic saga by sailing off into the sunset in his pure white canoe.

The way American Indians have appeared in much of American literature is nothing if not ironic. *The Song of Hiawatha,* the big daddy of them all, exemplifies that irony. To begin with, Longfellow got the name wrong. The stories told in his epic are about a culture hero of the Anishinabe, or Chippewa, people. The real Hiawatha was not Chippewa, but Iroquois. Hiawatha was a Mohawk leader who, with the Peacemaker, was one of the founders of the alliance of the Five Iroquois Nations: the Mohawk, Oneida, Onondaga, Cayuga, and Seneca. Called the Great League of Peace, that alliance deeply influenced both American Indian history and the eventual founding of the United States. For more than two centuries, the European powers had to deal with the Great League. Even the form of the United States Constitution appears to have borrowed directly from that of the League of the Iroquois—an influence acknowledged by such founding fathers as Benjamin Franklin.

Secondly, the character that Longfellow's *The Song of Hiawatha* is really about is Manabozho. Henry Rowe Schoolcraft, an Indian agent and a contemporary of Longfellow, was the source of Longfellow's information about American Indian myths. Schoolcraft's 1839 publication of *Algic Researches* drew attention to the fact that American Indians, who were viewed by many scholars as nothing but beasts, actually had an oral literature worthy of serious consideration. Schoolcraft's wife was a Chippewa Indian and the direct source of the stories he wrote down. However, even Schoolcraft toned those stories down considerably. The "real" Hiawatha is a full-blown Trickster, and many of his exploits were just as X-rated as those of Coyote. It could rightly be said that the bowdlerized Manabozho/Hiawatha memorialized by Longfellow has been dry-cleaned and then freeze-dried.

In 1956, the anthropologist Paul Radin published *The Trickster: A Study in American Indian Mythology,* a book that focused on the Trickster Cycle of the Winnebagos (today known by their own tribal name of Ho-Chunks). Here are some of the forty-nine episodes that Radin lists as part of the telling he records of the Winnebago Trickster Cycle:

> Trickster cohabits with women before a war party
> Trickster wishes to go on warpath alone
> Trickster makes his right arm fight his left
> Trickster borrows two children from his younger brother
> Children die because Trickster breaks rules
> Dancing ducks and talking anus
> Trickster burns anus and eats his own intestines
> Penis placed in box
> Changed into woman, Trickster marries chief's son

If you really want to understand American Indian cultures, then you have to understand the Trickster. Well, not really understand. Not only is that too academic, it is rather unlikely. So, let's just say accept. Accept the possibilities and the reality of Trickster and you have made a big step. True, it may be off a cliff, but you can always learn from a fall as long as it isn't too big a one.

Coyote is the biggest fool of all. I've heard that said by many different American Indian people over the years. Yet Coyote is just as often acknowledged as a defender of the people, a shaper of the Earth itself, one with godlike power. Coyote not only fools himself, he also makes fools out of the monsters that threaten the people. He is a strange mixture—part culture hero and part buffoon. Even when his mistakes end catastrophically—to the point of his death and dismemberment—Coyote always comes back to life again. Further, Coyote and all the other Tricksters—including Spider (Iktomi), Great Rabbit, Raven, and others—are also Changers. They change themselves, and not just from animal to human. They can change their age, their sex, make themselves seem to be a bird or a stone.

Further, they are shapers of the Earth and its beings. Many things today are the way they are (for better or worse) because of Coyote. There are so many stories of Coyote's foolish or heroic behavior that Jarold Ramsey was able to publish a thick volume of such traditional tales, *Coyote Was Going There* (1977), from the tribal nations of Oregon alone.

The first of the stories in Ramsey's collection, "Coyote and the Swallowing Monster," is a classic example of how Coyote and similar culture heroes throughout the continent make fools out of powerful and terrible beings. First published in Nez Perce Texts (1934) by the Nez Perce writer Archie Finnie, whose primary source was his own mother, Wayi'larpu, the story begins in the time before human beings are created. Coyote is making a fish ladder (at what would be Celilo Falls on the Columbia River in the Pacific Northwest) so that the fish will be able to go upstream for people to catch. Coyote learns that a great monster in the shape of a hill has swallowed all the animal people by sucking them in. Coyote takes a bath and dresses himself up to make himself appear more appetizing to the monster. He puts a pack on his back with five stone knives, some pitch, and a flint fire-making set. Then he challenges the monster to a contest to see which of them can inhale the other. Coyote goes first, drawing in his breath noisily. Of course, he fails. Then he says to the monster, "You have swallowed all the people; now swallow me, too, unless I become lonely." Of course, that is what the monster does. Inside its body Coyote finds the other animal people and he asks them to help him find the creature's heart. He makes a fire, then starts cutting away at the heart with his stone knives, eventually killing the monster. He then cuts up the monster and casts parts of its flesh all over the land, "toward the sunrise, toward the sunset, toward the warmth, toward the cold," where those parts of the monster's body become the various Indian nations.

Then there is the widespread tale of the eye juggler. In one Northern Paiute version, we see a Coyote as easily fooled as the monsters he overcomes. Coyote comes across Wildcat and Skunk playing a game in which they take out their eyes, throw them up into the air, and then hold back their heads so that their eyes fall back into place (just as in certain Lakota stories about Iktomi and the Pueblo tale of Skeleton Woman). Coyote immediately wants to try it. He pulls his eyes out, throws them up, leans his head back, and they fall into place. Everyone laughs, and so he tries it again, throwing them higher each time. The last time he tries it, Wildcat knocks the eyes to one side with a stick. Then Skunk and Wildcat run away, taking Coyote's eyes with them. Eventually, after a number of adventures, Coyote gets his eyes back. Sometimes they are not his original ones, though. In versions told by the White Mountain and Chiricahua Apaches, Coyote is given eyes made of pine pitch. As a result, his eyes are yellow to this day. His vision, such as it is, is restored, and Coyote continues on, no wiser than before.

Although Coyote is the best-known exemplar of the Trickster in Native North American culture, with Coyote stories stretching in a broad band from the Southwest through the Plains, the Great Basin, and California up into the Pacific Northwest, he (or she) is far from alone. Among other peoples of the Northwest we have Raven (or sometimes Crow), who is the primary Trickster/Changer among the Indians and Inuits of Alaska and the Pacific Northwest. Among the Crees and many of the other northern peoples of the Canadian inland, the Trickster is called Wisakijak. (Although the popular name for the Canada jay, also called the "camp robber," is Whiskey Jack, this is probably just a result of the similarity between the Cree word for the jay, which is *wiskacanis,* and the Cree Trickster's name *wisahkicahk.* The latter Cree word, but not the former, has *wisak,* meaning "bitter" or "suffer," at its root.) In the Great Plains we find that

trickster's turn

Iktomi among the Lakotas and Veho, or Wihio among the Cheyennes, is identified as a spider. Among the eastern woodlands peoples, such nations as the Anishinabe, the Ho-Chunk, the Menominee, and others have the one who is known by such names as Nanabush, Winebojo, or Manabozho and is frequently identified with Rabbit. Rabbit is also the crafty hero of most of the Trickster cycles of the southeastern tribal nations, including the Cherokee.

In every case, the hero/fool alternates between being Promethean and pathetic. He may be the savior of the people or a horrible example of how humans should not behave. Since the respect of others is one of the most important things to have in all American Indian cultures—much more important than material possessions—it is easy to see how the misdeeds of such hero/fools as Coyote and the others both reinforce cultural norms by breaking them and provide a kind of vicarious delight to those who hear about someone doing all the things one should never do. The tales admonish the listeners while allowing them to take imaginative part in every possible cultural taboo.

Also, although Trickster may fool others, those who listen to a Trickster story are not fooled. Part of it is because, knowing they are going to hear, for example, a story about Coyote, they are prepared right from the start. Then there are ways of telling the story, including the language itself, that let listeners in on the joke. Take Coyote's voice. I've heard Coyote stories told in a number of American Indian languages that I don't speak, but I've known as soon as Coyote starts talking who it is that I am listening to because his voice is highly nasalized. American Indian audiences all over the continent find it amusing and a dead giveaway that we're dealing with a Trickster when that nasal voice is heard in a story. With that long nose of his, how else could he sound when he talks? In a similar way, the Shoshone Bear's voice is slower and deeper than Coyote's and often is growled as much as it is spoken. Like the more recently legendary traveling salesman (although we might make a case for that being one legitimate interpretation of the way Trickster approaches his gullible foils), Coyote is literally a fast talker. Further, in some American Indian languages, there are actual words (or nonsense syllables) spoken by Coyote and no one else. For example, in Shoshone, when Coyote talks, he not only does so haltingly, he also ends his sentences with *pai*. (And now you finally know where all those *pais* came from in the story at the start of Chapter Four.)

Interestingly enough, not only does nasalization of the Trickster's voice occur in many American Indian nations (for Raven and Veho and Iktomi and Raccoon and Rabbit), it also may be found in traditional Trickster stories on other continents. While I was living and teaching in Ghana, forty years ago, when I was told Ewe stories of Yiyi the Spider and Twi tales of Anansi the Spider, Spider's voice was nasalized.

Paul Radin's classic volume, *The Trickster,* mentioned above, has at its core the Trickster stories of the Ho-Chunk. Here is one such tale:

trickster's black shirt

Trickster is out walking around near a lake one afternoon when he sees someone standing on the other side of the lake. That person is wearing a black shirt and pointing his arm at him. Pointing at someone in this way is rude behavior and it offends Trickster.

"Stop that, Younger Brother," Trickster says. But the one pointing at him does not stop. This makes Trickster angry.

"I, too, can play this game," Trickster says. Then he goes home, puts on a black shirt, and comes back to stand with his own arm pointing at that rude person. Trickster stands that way all through the night. When the sun comes up the next day, the morning light shows Trickster that what he thought was someone pointing at him was actually a one-limbed dead tree blackened by fire.

"It is because I do things like this that the people call me the Foolish One," Trickster says. *"They are right."*

These stories of foolish behaviors are so popular and widespread that virtually the same tale sometimes turns up in different Native cultures with their own foolish hero as protagonist. Take the story of Manabozho/Iktomi/Veho and the Ducks. I've personally heard tellings by Lakota, Anishinabe, and Cheyenne people, and I've read numerous written versions of the tale from those and other Native nations. In the first part of the narrative, the Trickster plays the role of clever deceiver, luring the ducks into his lodge for a dance, telling them to dance with their eyes closed so that the smoke of his fire will not redden their eyes, and then strangling them one by one. In the second half of the story, however, when Trickster goes to cook those ducks, making an outdoor pit fire, covering the ducks with clay and then burying them with only their legs sticking out, his own foolishness defeats him.

Whenever one of these classic culture hero Trickster fools gets into trouble, it is inevitably the result of anger, acquisitiveness, stupidity—or all three together. Take, for example, another Ho-Chunk story:

trickster's hands

Trickster was eating. Only one piece of meat remained on his plate. He reached for it with both hands. His right hand grabbed one side of that piece of meat and his left hand grabbed the other.

"This meat is mine," said his right hand.

"No, it is mine," said his left hand.

Trickster tried to stop them, but his hands would not listen. They began to struggle over that piece of meat. They tugged back and forth. Finally his hands got so angry that they attacked each other with knives. The scars from that fight can be seen as the lines on every person's palms.

What could be more stupid than two hands fighting over food being carried to the same mouth? It is as senseless as a similar sort of anger and selfishness between people in the same family or the same village. Spurred on by blind greed, it leaves scars on all of us. How perfect a story it is, not just about Coyote or Manabozho or Iktomi, but about all of humanity.

Trickster's failings, of course, are the exact equivalents of the three classic destroyers in Buddhist philosophy—the hatred, greed, and delusion that humans must free themselves from before they can be either truly happy or enlightened beings. Bearing that in mind, it is easy to see the reasons why such stories are not just popular, but of central importance. Teaching by negative example, they reinforce the very cultural norms that their foolish heroes ignore: *Don't be like Coyote when he is that way.*

But we are. And so it is among contemporary American Indian people that we have many stories of people who play the fool just as well as Trickster does. Unlike the Coyote Trickster, who may seem immoral or at least amoral in his foolishness, the fools in these contemporary stories are often admirable or well-meaning people. They do foolish things and suffer consequences, but the stories told about them are told with a certain fondness. Further, these contemporary fools are real people, not figures who could be described (by ethnologists, if not Native people themselves) as mythic or archetypal. In some ways, the stories have a sort of leveling effect, keeping people who might otherwise be elevated because of their status or their special abilities at the same human level as everyone else. Part of the reasons why these stories lead us to sympathize with their protagonists is that they often end with the one who has been foolish laughing at himself. One of my favorite of such real-life characters is a Micmac man named Louis Tomah, who lived in northern Maine in the first half of the twentieth century.

Laughing Louie was the name most knew him by. The Micmacs of Aroostook County, Maine, still tell stories about Laughing Louie. In *The Wabanakis of Maine and the Maritimes* (prepared for and published by the American Friends Service Committee in 1989) he is mentioned in the reminiscences of half a dozen Micmac people who knew him in the 1930s and 1940s. Louie was a large man, but though he had great strength, he was remembered as gentle and kind. He had the sort of generosity that meant, as one person put it, "he couldn't keep a penny in his pockets because there was always somebody else who needed that penny more than he did." He walked everywhere, camping out in the woods. People never knew when Louie would turn up, seemingly out of nowhere. The first thing they always heard was his laughter. When Louie did foolish things that would make others angry or even despairing, he would laugh. People might laugh at the foolish things he did, but Louie laughed with them. Here is one well-known story of Laughing Louie:

the car that really hummed along

It was the end of potato-picking time around the town of Limestone. Louie had shown up to join in the work and now he was getting ready to go. Someone had an old junk car that had been left out all summer near the fields. They told Louie he could take it if he could get it going.

"I'll have it humming along in no time," Louie said.

But when he got in and tried to start it up by rolling it downhill, he stirred up a swarm of hornets that had made their nest under the seat. When he tried to get out, the door wouldn't work. He was stuck in there getting stung until he reached the bottom of the hill. By the time he got out he was black and blue and his eyes were swollen shut—but he was laughing. He was laughing and laughing. The whole town of Limestone shook with his laughter.

"Boy," Louie said, "that car really hummed along!"

Then he laughed some more.

My Cheyenne friend Lance Henson loves telling stories of contemporary people who do such things. A few years ago Lance told me about a young man who felt he needed to do a sweat lodge, that basic purification ceremony in which a small round lodge is erected, heated stones are brought inside, the lodge door is closed, and then water is poured over the red-hot stones, filling the lodge with steam.

the telephone pole sweat

There was an elder who was known for doing sweat lodges for those who needed them. The man went to that elder's house, but the elder wasn't home. He was away on a long trip. The elder's brother was there, however. Even though the brother didn't usually do such things, he decided to take pity on the young man.

"I will help you," he said. "You come back tomorrow evening and I'll have the lodge ready."

After the young man left, though, the brother forgot all about what he had promised. He didn't remember until it was the middle of the next day. Still, he told himself it would be all right because there was time to get everything ready. All he had to do was cover the lodge and build the fire to heat the stones. But when he went to the woodpile, he saw that he had a problem. All the wood had been used up. He had a chain saw, but there were no trees close by and he didn't have time to drive to the nearest place where he could get more wood.

Then he remembered something. Oklahoma Bell had dumped a bunch of old telephone poles down by the road. He took his chain saw and cut the poles into lengths and split them with his ax. They were good and dry, and when he started the fire they got really hot really fast. By the time the young man showed up, the stones were heated.

"Everything is ready," the brother said. "We can go into the lodge."

So they took off their clothes and went into the lodge. They did their sweat. The stones were brought in and the water was poured. In the heat of the lodge they prayed, and everything went well until they opened the lodge door and looked at each other. There had been creosote in those telephone poles, so much that when the water was poured on the rocks, the steam that rose had creosote in it. Those two men were black from head to toe.

The brother started laughing. "Well," he said, "it looks like we just had an Amos and Andy sweat."

Several of the Apache groups have a "Foolish People" genre of stories in which the main characters are Apaches who seem to have learned nothing about the right way to behave as a true Apache. Although the Apaches proved themselves to be among the most determined and brilliant tacticians of guerilla warfare in human history, the Foolish People found in Lipan, Jicarilla, and Chiricahua stories do one dumb, even life-threatening thing after another. My old friend Swift Eagle, whose grandfather was Jicarilla Apache, loved to tell stories about two (or three—the number varied) such Foolish People who were brothers. Their names were Foot, Foot-Foot, and Foot-Foot-Foot. Here is a brief telling of a Foolish People story that the ethnologist Morris Opler heard seventy years ago from the Chiricahuas:

the camp of foolish people

There was a camp of Foolish People. They placed it right out in the open so that it could be easily found. One day the white soldiers came to their camp. The Foolish People went out to greet them and the soldiers started shooting at them.

"You are welcome," one Foolish Person said. The soldiers shot him.

"Why are these soldiers shooting us?" one Foolish Person said to another Foolish Person. The soldiers shot them both.

A group of Foolish People went up to the soldiers. "Why are you shooting us?" they asked. The soldiers shot them, too.

The soldiers kept shooting and shooting. Finally an old man of the Foolish People got an idea. "I think we should run away," he said.

"That is a good idea," said the survivors. And so they did.

Just like Coyote stories, such tales offer powerful lessons—in this case, the inadvisability of trusting outsiders too much by offering a ridiculous reverse example. This story in particular is doubly powerful, for while the Chiricahuas were laughing at the foolish behavior of those people who didn't know enough to run, they were also reminding themselves of the absolute ruthlessness of American or Mexican soldiers who often massacred Apaches. American Indian humor can be hard for outsiders to grasp. Sometimes it is because there are so many commonly understood things among Indians that we laugh when others don't. (Sherman Alexie, the brilliant young Spokane/Coeur D'Alene poet and novelist, adapted some of his work for the screen, resulting in the much-praised movie *Smoke Signals,* about present-day reservation life. Although the movie has been enthusiastically received by white audiences, there are places in it where the Indians in the audience laugh and the whites don't. Alexie calls those moments "Indian trapdoors.") And sometimes it is hard for a non-Indian to understand why things as grim as massacres could be subjects for humor. Here is an Abenaki story, based on a real event in New England history, that offers an example of the kind of Indian humor that may make white audiences cringe:

exactly five pounds

B*ack about two hundred years ago, there was a trading post along the Connecticut River called Fort Number Four. The Abenakis brought their furs in to trade them at that fort. But there was a problem. The trader at the fort didn't like Indians, and the Abenakis suspected he was dealing unfairly and cheating them. They were paid for their skins by weight, and the trader used a balance scale. He would place the skins on one side and then place his right hand on the other.*

"My hand weighs exactly five pounds," he would say. It was amazing how many skins it took to weigh five pounds when he did that. If any Indian protested, the trader would pull out the club he kept behind his counter and beat him with it. He was not the only white man who treated the Indians badly, and the Indians' resentment grew.

Finally, the time came when the Abenakis could no longer accept the treatment they were receiving. They attacked Fort Number Four and wiped out the white men.

After the battle was over, two Abenaki men were walking around when they came to the wreckage of the trading post. There lay the body of the white trader they had always suspected of cheating them. And right next to him, tipped over but unbroken, were his balance scales.

The two Abenakis looked at each other.

"My friend," the first one said, "I just happen to have a five-pound weight here in my pack."

"Let us find out then," said the second man.

So they cut off the trader's right hand. They set the scales up and placed the five-pound weight in one tray. Then they placed the trader's hand in the other. And they felt really bad when they discovered that the white man's hand did, in fact, weigh exactly five pounds.

How can death and dismemberment be funny? Trickster offers an explanation of this with another aspect of Coyote and his cousins that I haven't mentioned yet. You can find it in the widespread Northwest Coast tale of Raven and Octopus Woman. (A really wonderful telling of this story by the Nootka/Saanich storyteller Johnny Moses can be found on his audiotape *Octopus Lady and Crow*.) Raven is warned by one creature after another not to go down to the tide pools where Octopus Woman is lurking. Of course he ignores the warnings and goes straight there. Octopus Woman lures him closer and closer by flattering him. When he is close enough, she grabs him with her tentacles and holds him until he drowns in the rising tide. But the story doesn't really end there. After his death, Raven comes back to life again.

Although a Trickster may die, he or she often shows the power to revive himself or herself—just as Coyote does when he is crushed by a rolling rock in a Pawnee tale or falls from a great height in the Laguna Pueblo story retold in a memorable poem by Leslie Marmon Silko. Coyote and his relatives make themselves into a chain down the face of a cliff by holding each other's tails in their mouths so that Coyote can be lowered down to steal some food. Naturally, since it is the most inappropriate thing to do, one of the coyotes farts. "Who did that?" says the coyote at the top of the cliff, letting go of the tail of the coyote beneath him. Then all of them fall to their deaths on the rocks below.

What happens when Tricksters meet each other? Here's one example, the Plains Cree tale of how Coyote ran into Wisakijak. (This is a logical encounter, since of all the creatures on this continent, the only native animal that has managed to increase its range since the coming of Europeans is Coyote. On moonlit winter nights here in the Adirondack Mountains of New York, where the wolf ranged a century ago, I now hear packs of coyotes singing from the ridges of Glass Factory Mountain behind our cabin. In fact, in many traditional tales where the main Trickster figure is not Coyote, a coyote still wanders into the narrative.)

the older brother

One day Wisakijak was out walking around when he ran into Coyote.

"Hello, Younger Brother," Wisakijak said.

"No," said Coyote, "I should say that. I am older than you. You are my Younger Brother."

"That is not true," Wisakijak replied. "I am older."

The two of them argued back and forth about that. Neither one could prove that he was older. Finally they had an idea. Old people die before young people.

"If one of us is older than the other, then surely the one who is oldest will die first," Wisakijak said.

"That is true," said Coyote.

"Then let us have a contest," said Wisakijak. "The first one to die of old age will lose. Then the winner can be called Older Brother."

"That is good," said Coyote. "I like contests. I will surely win."

So the two of them sat down across from each other, waiting to see who would die first. They waited and waited, neither of them saying anything. Winter came and went.

"Have you died yet?" Wisakijak said.

"No," Coyote answered. "Have you?"

So they sat there through more winters. Every two years one of them would ask if the other was dead. Each time the answer was no, and so they kept sitting there.

Finally, one spring, Wisakijak asked the question again. "Have you died yet?"

Coyote did not answer. He sat there with his eyes closed.

"Hah!" Wisakijak shouted, jumping to his feet. "I have won. I am the Older Brother."

Coyote opened his eyes. "That's the trouble with you young people these days," he said. "You got no patience."

Then Coyote ran away before Wisakijak could kill him.

Life and death are equally mutable. They are equally serious, equally ridiculous, and also equally sacred. Trickster never really dies for good, and his lesson about the interchangeable nature of even death and life is a profound one for us all. Dangerous and beautiful, the master of mimicry and birth, glib, deceitful, untrustworthy, yet reliable. No being more than Trickster embodies the chaotic, ever-flowing, and thus potentially creative nature of life itself. Like a heavy stone lifted and held over your head, that energy is stored and may be released simply by letting it fall. The one constant is change. So it is that Coyote, the Trickster, the Changer, is always with us. Everything is impermanent. Death just as much so as life. In the long run, difficult as the world may be, it is a lot less grim with Trickster in it—even if the universe is still, inevitably, as mysterious and illogical as Coyote.

To understand Indians, Old Man says, you have to understand Coyote.
   Hey, Coyote says, no one understands me.
   Exactly my point, Old Man replies.

Recommended Reading

King, Thomas (Cherokee). *Medicine River.* New York: Laurel Press, 1990. The character of Harlan Bigbear, meddler extraordinaire, is one of the funniest manipulators in modern fiction and one reason why this episodic novel about life on a modern Canadian reservation is so delightful. (The book was also made into a very good movie of the same name.)

Ortiz, Alfonso (Pueblo), and Erdoes, Richard, eds. and comps. *American Indian Trickster Tales.* New York: Pantheon Books, 1998. This collection of Trickster stories, old and new, from more than sixty different tribal nations around the continent, is one of the best introductions to this important genre of American Indian traditions.

Ramsey, Jarold, ed. and comp. *Coyote Was Going There: Indian Literature of the Oregon Country.* Seattle: University of Washington Press, 1977. Few collections of traditional tales are as well put together and carefully presented as this book, which gives a wonderful picture of the oral traditions of Oregon and has been extremely useful to both Native and non-Native storytellers.

Vizenor, Gerald (Chippewa). *The Trickster of Liberty.* Minneapolis: University of Minnesota Press, 1988. This novel is only one of many by Vizenor in which he draws on the Trickster tradition. More than any other American Indian author, Vizenor celebrates and identifies with this protean protagonist.

Sign language

I am like a bear
I hold my hands
waiting for the sun to rise

—*Pawnee Song*

Sign language was not limited to the Plains Indians. It appears to have been used all over the continent, even though local forms of sign language seem to have been abandoned a generation or two after the first contact with Europeans by the Native nations of the Southeast and Northeast. However, Delaware Indian scouts (whose original Munsee homeland is the area of the Hudson Valley of New York, New Jersey, and Pennsylvania) fluent in the use of sign language guided several generations of explorers across the West, and a large number of the Delaware people ended up in Oklahoma.

The most widely known of American Indian sign languages, that of the Great Plains, was easily understood by a great many different tribal nations. In 1881, recognizing its importance, General William T. Sherman directed one of his soldiers to compile a manual for use by his army officers. That man was Second Lieutenant William Philo Clark, who had been taught Indian sign language by none other than Oh Kom Ha Ka, the Cheyenne headman of the Elk Society, who was known to the whites as Little Wolf. Clark's book *The Indian Sign Language* was published in 1885. It was followed by several other publications on sign language by other authors. The best of those, *Indian Sign Language*, by William Tomkins, who learned sign primarily from the Lakotas of Montana, was published in 1931 and remains in print through Dover Books.

Sign Language

The importance of Indian sign language was recognized by Europeans long before Sherman's directive. Early knowledge of Indian sign language and the use of English-speaking Indian translators fluent in signing made it possible for white explorers and trappers to communicate quite adequately with dozens of different tribal nations while knowing nothing of their spoken languages. Those Delaware Indian scouts, such as Black Beaver, are only one example. The most notable use of Indian sign talkers occurred with the Lewis and Clark Expedition (1803–1806). George Drouillard, whose mother was Shawnee, was described by both Lewis and Clark as the best man in their company. This deeply reliable man was invaluable to the success of their mission, not only due to his considerable prowess as a hunter and outdoorsman, but because of his ability as a sign talker as the white men encountered tribe after tribe whose language was unknown to anyone in their party.

Although sign language has largely been replaced by English as the means of communication between different tribal nations, it can still be found in use among contemporary Indians. You may see it in use at powwows or other gatherings—perhaps when an Indian recites the Lord's Prayer, singing it in English while simultaneously interpreting it in sign. It is not uncommon to this day in Oklahoma, where so many tribal nations ended up, to see Indians from different tribes talking to one another in English or their different Native languages and signing at the same time.

I have been taught sign language by several elders from western and southwestern tribes over the years, and I sometimes use sign language myself when I am doing storytelling programs or poetry readings throughout the continent. I have had older Indians of various tribes come up to me after those programs to say how much they enjoyed seeing, as a Tlingit elder in Alaska said to me, "someone using our old trade language."

contact: the coming of europeans

WHY WILL YOU TAKE FROM US BY FORCE WHAT YOU CAN OBTAIN BY

LOVE? WHY WILL YOU DESTROY US WHO SUPPLY YOU WITH FOOD?

WHAT CAN YOU GET BY WAR? WE ARE UNARMED AND WILLING TO

GIVE YOU WHAT YOU ASK IF YOU COME IN A FRIENDLY MANNER.

—*Wahunsunacock (Powhatan), 1609*

a friend of the indians

(SENECA)

There was a man who was known as a friend of the Indians. One day, Red Jacket invited that man to walk with him. The two of them walked together until they came to a log by the river.

"Let us sit together," Red Jacket said.

So the two of them sat on the log, but after a short time Red Jacket slid closer to the white man.

"Move over," Red Jacket said.

The man did as Red Jacket asked, but before long Red Jacket again slid over on the log.

"Move over," he said again.

Just as before, the man slid over. And, just as before, Red Jacket again slid over on the log and asked the man to move. Even though he was now getting very close to the end of the log that hung out over the water, the white man did as Red Jacket said.

Then Red Jacket slid over a fourth time. "Move over," he said once more.

"But if I go any farther," the white man replied, "I shall fall into the water."

"Ah," said Red Jacket, "and even so your people tell us to move on when there is nowhere left to go."

welcome, friends

W*hat cheer, netop. Kwai nidoba. Wingapo.*

When the Europeans came to our land, we welcomed them. We find this not only in our oral histories but in the written records of European explorers and colonists. The words for "Welcome" or "Hello, my friends" were usually the first uttered by Native Americans to the pale-skinned aliens—unless the newcomers attacked them before words could be spoken.

By November 11, 1620, when the *Mayflower* landed on the Massachusetts coast, the Native people of the region had learned to be wary of the strangers from the sea. They had every reason for caution. The white people carried dangerous new weapons. They were tense and excitable enough to shoot first in any situation that seemed uncertain. Some white visitors to those shores had been duplicitous, pretending friendship and then abducting Native people. Worst of all, the coming of the whites was often followed by such new diseases as smallpox, measles, and influenza, which swept through the Native communities like an uncontrollable fire.

The first Indian to speak to the Pilgrims of Massachusetts was an Abenaki named Samoset. On March 16, 1621, he walked into Plymouth Plantation and actually greeted them in their own language by saying "Welcome, Englishmen."

Samoset was not from that part of the New England coast, which is the homeland of the Wampanoags, but was visiting friends there. It was, however, Samoset who introduced the Pilgrims to another Indian man who was very much a native of that area. In fact, the Pilgrims had chosen to place their settlement where Squanto's now-vanished village of Pawtuxet had been. Although the Pilgrims did not know it at the time, the wide fields of "virgin land" around their new settlement had been cleared by the Pawtuxets, who had nearly all died from one of those epidemics. The virgin land of New England was actually widowed earth.

That Pawtuxet Wampanoag man brought by Samoset to the Pilgrims was known as Tisquantum, or Squanto. Tisquantum had been kidnapped eight years before, along with nineteen other Pawtuxet men, by an English captain named Thomas Hunt, who had invited them on board his ship for a friendly dinner. Hunt then clapped them in irons and took them to Spain, where they were sold as slaves. Amazingly, Tisquantum gained his freedom and found his way to England, where he was employed by the Newfoundland Company as an interpreter, sailing with them to North America. He made at least one other trip back and forth to North America before his final return to his own homeland just about the same time as the arrival of the Pilgrims. Imagine, if you can, how this man felt when he returned home at last, after having been taken as a slave, to find his village gone, his parents and wife and family all dead. If this were a Hollywood movie, starring the Indian equivalent of Bruce Willis or Arnold Schwarzenegger, the next scene would be our hero arming himself to the teeth and then wiping out the foreign villains responsible for his losses.

Instead, Tisquantum became the savior of Plymouth Plantation. He acted as interpreter between them and the nearby Wampanoag villages led by Massasoit. He showed them how to plant their crops and live off the land. He stayed a friend of the Pilgrims until he became ill and died, in Plymouth Plantation, two years later. We can never know all of Tisquantum's motives for becoming a friend of the Pilgrims. In part, it may have been his desire to remain on the land that he loved as one loves one's mother. He had lived in England, where he saw just how many white people there were—unlike the other Indians, who had never left North America and sometimes assumed that there were not all that many Europeans in the world. Thus, he may have made the purely pragmatic decision to ally himself with the English because he recognized that they were too many and too powerful to fight. It is certainly true that other American Indian nations—including the Mohegans in Connecticut and the Crows of the Great Plains—would choose not to fight the whites but to help them in their wars against other American Indian nations. Intertribal warfare and the making of alliances to fight other enemy nations were common practices in pre-Columbian North and South America. Tisquantum also may have been trying to bring back together those remaining Pawtuxets who had been adopted into the other Wampanoag villages. Tisquantum's unsuccessful attempts to gain more political power among the Wampanoags, perhaps even to the point of hoping to overthrow Massasoit, led to his taking refuge among the Pilgrims to escape Massasoit's wrath.

Whatever the reasons, the story of Tisquantum is also the story of a man who helped those people who came from the same nation that had enslaved him and caused the loss of his family, his village, his entire world. It might be interpreted as a story of forgiveness on a truly monumental scale, an example of the way American Indians tried to accommodate Europeans and bring them into their world. It might be seen as setting that pattern of welcoming immigrants for which the new nation of the United States would be known.

As the early contact period went on, Indian communities became more concerned about these new people. Their lack of respect and their increasing numbers—as ship after ship brought more of them to our shores—were troubling to our ancestors. (When American Indians hear white Americans complain about "illegal aliens," we sometimes feel like reminding them that for us the problem started in 1492.) These boat people were unlike anyone else we had ever encountered.

A similar problem faced every Native nation as the Europeans spread out over the continent, and a study of the names given to white people is like a study of Indian/white relations. Lance Henson, my Cheyenne friend, explained to me why his people call the whites "Veho." Veho is the old name for the protagonist of many Cheyenne lesson stories, a Trickster figure whose life is ruled by his uncontrolled appetites and his quarrelsome, irrational nature. Also, like the Anansi figure of the West African Akan nations, Veho is a spider, the black widow spider, to be precise. "The black widow spider," Lance said, "is very beautiful to look at. That is how we saw those white people. They were beautiful. But they were deadly if you let them get too close."

the gifts of the black robes

The first white people to come were often missionaries. They brought Christian teachings that resonated with the philosophies of a great many tribal nations. Many of these missionaries, in particular the French Jesuits, were accomplished linguists who studied and wrote down tribal languages. The missionaries also recorded vivid descriptions of traditional Native cultures, even though those reports were often colored by ethnocentrism. *The Jesuit Relations*—reports sent over the course of three centuries by the Jesuit priests back to their superiors in France—are an incredibly important archive of life among such people as the Hurons, Abenakis, and other Indians of "New France."

The Jesuits were good observers and attempted, despite their cultural bias, to describe things accurately and honestly. One story from the 1636 *Relation* of Jean de Brebeuf is an interesting example of the Huron attitudes toward these new medicine people, whom they called Black Robes, and who were sometimes suspected of engaging in black magic. A drought had come, and a Huron *arendiwane* (medicine man) attempted to bring the rain through his usual ritual, which included dreaming and dance. When the rain did not come, the *arendiwane* said it was the fault of the Black Robes, that the blood-red cross they had placed beside their door was blocking his power. They must take it down, or be killed as sorcerers. Things grew very tense in the village until the Jesuits brought the people together and told them they could make it rain through their Christian prayers to God. Their cross should not be taken down because it would help them pray. When the rain actually did come after the Jesuits prayed (fortunately for them!), a number of the Hurons became convinced of the usefulness of this new way of praying.

Many American Indians embraced Christianity. But, more often than not, they did it and continue to do it with their eyes open—with good reason. There is a poignant saying about the coming of the whites with Christianity. Like many of the stories about Indians and whites, it has been recorded in more than one tribal nation around the continent: "When the whites first came, they had the Bible and we had the land." I've also heard it expressed in the form of a poem, whose author remains anonymous:

The white men told me
to bow my head and pray.
And while I did this,
they took my land away.

(This experience is one that is truly intertribal among people who have been subjected to European colonization. While I was a volunteer teacher in Ghana, West Africa, my attention was called to a very similar poem written in pidgin English by a Nigerian.)

Yet another widespread comment, which has been attributed to any number of American Indians past and present, is that "Jesus must have been an Indian." If one asks why, one is given a long list of the ways in which the teachings of Christ correspond much more closely with Native traditions than they do with European actions, ending with the fact that they crucified him. Much to their chagrin, even the early Jesuit missionaries who were attempting to instruct the "savages" often found themselves recording the fact that such Christian virtues as charity and kindness were much more common among the Natives than among the Europeans. The many volumes of *The Jesuit Relations,* translated into English by Reuben Gold Thwaites, are filled with such testimonies as the following from a letter sent in 1636 by a Jesuit father living among the Iroquois:

Hospitals for the poor would be useless among them, because there are no beggars; those who have are so liberal to those who are in want, that everything is enjoyed in common. The whole village must be in distress before any individual is left in necessity.

One of the most famous responses to Christian proselytizing was made in 1805 in Buffalo, New York, by the Seneca elder Red Jacket, a man widely recognized as one of the most eloquent orators of his day. The power of his delivery, the logic of his message, his wit, and his beautiful, resonant voice drew both white and Indian alike whenever word went out that Red Jacket was to speak. On this particular occasion, a missionary named Reverend Cram spoke to the assembled Indians about giving up their heathen ways and turning to the one true religion. After he finished, the Iroquois conferred for about two hours by themselves before Red Jacket returned to give their reply. Among the telling points he made in his response were these:

> Brother, our seats were once large, and yours were very small; you have now become a great people, and we have scarcely a place left to spread our blankets; you have got our country, but are not satisfied; you want to force your religion upon us.
>
> Brother, continue to listen. You say that you are sent to instruct us to worship the Great Spirit agreeably to His mind, and if we do not take hold of the religion which you White people teach, we shall be unhappy hereafter; you say you know this is right and we are lost; how do we know this to be true? We understand that your religion is written in a book; if it was intended for us as well as you, why has not the Great Spirit given it to us, and not only to us, but why did He not give to our forefathers the knowledge of that book, with the means of understanding it rightly? We only know what you tell us about it; how shall we know what to believe, being so often deceived by the White people?
>
> Brother, you say there is but one way to worship and serve the Great Spirit; if there is but one religion, why do you White people differ so much about it? Why not all agree, as all can read the book?

Further, Red Jacket pointed out that the Iroquois had their own religion given them by their forefathers, but they had no wish to force it upon others. "Brother," Red Jacket said, "we do not wish to destroy your religion, or take it from you. We want only to enjoy our own." His final point was the most telling and is an example of the incisiveness of Red Jacket's logic. I suspect that more than one of the Indians assembled tried hard to keep a straight face when he concluded that:

> ...we are told you have been preaching to White people in this place; these people are our neighbors, we are acquainted with them; we will wait a little while and see what effect your preaching has upon them. If we find that it does them good, makes them honest and less disposed to cheat Indians, we will then consider again what you have said.
>
> Brother, you have now heard our answer to your talk, and this is all we have to say at present. As we are going to part, we will come and take you by the hand, and hope the Great Spirit will protect you on your journey, and return you safe to your friends.

However, when the Indians approached the missionary, Reverend Cram turned away and refused to take their hands, saying, "There is no fellowship between the religion of God and the works of the Devil."

When his words were interpreted to Red Jacket and the others, it is reported that "they smiled and retired in a peaceable manner." (The previous two extracts and related quotes are from Book V, Chapter VII, of *Book of the Indians,* by Sam G. Drake, published in 1836.)

Not only did the Indians never made an attempt to convert white men, but from the very start of the colonial period a great many white men willingly tried to join the Indians. During the first months of the Jamestown Colony, the Powhatan Indians returned—after feeding them and treating them with great kindness—a number of white men and boys who had run away from the settlement to one Powhatan village or another. Laws were passed in the early days of Plymouth forbidding white men and women to interact or live with the

Indians. For the next four centuries the phenomenon of whites choosing to become as Indian as they possibly could would occur wherever European people came in contact with Native Americans. This pattern of "going Native" became established so early on that Sir Francis Bacon, one of Shakespeare's seventeenth-century contemporaries, made the following observation, as recorded in *The Gospel of the Redman* (compiled by Ernest Thompson Seton and Julia M. Seton):

> It hath often been seen that a Christian gentleman, well-born and bred, and gently nurtured, will, of his own will, quit his high status and luxurious world, to dwell with savages and live their lives, taking part in all their savagery. But never yet hath it been seen that a savage will, of his own free will, give up his savagery and live the life of a civilized man.

As Ohiyesa, the Dakota Sioux writer whose European name was Charles Eastman, would observe almost three centuries later in his classic autobiography, *Indian Boyhood* (1902), "What boy would not want to be an Indian." Or what man?

No one has done a better job of discussing American Indian religious practice in relation to Christianity than the Lakota philosopher Vine Deloria, Jr., a man who might be seen as the modern-day Red Jacket. Deloria's *God Is Red* should be required reading for anyone who seeks a deeper understanding of the way our Native people relate to the Creator. It also points out the kind of dead end that religious hypocrisy has created for those who espouse Christianity and then practice its opposite.

Christian stories and teachings have entered American Indian life and may be found reflected in many ways. In some cases, as in the following tale narrated by Piudy, a Western Paiute Indian of Oregon, an ancient Judeo-Christian story may be seen through Indian eyes in a very new and pointed way.

the coming of the white people

(PAIUTE)

In the old days everything was Coyote's Way.
Then the apple tree was planted
and all the people were told, "Come and eat."
Hearing that, all the people came.
The white man was a rattlesnake then;
white men still have eyes like the rattlesnake.
When the Indians tried to eat the apple,
that rattlesnake tried to bite them.
That's why the white people took everything
away from the Indians—because they were snakes.
Just because they were snakes and came here
the white people took everything away.
They asked those Indians where they had come from.
They told the Indians to go away,
way out into the mountains to live.

name-calling

Thinking of how Europeans saw Indians and how Indians in turn saw Europeans brings us to the question of names. I do not know of anyplace in the world where more people have been misnamed or given new names than American Indians were. First, European "discoverers" claimed and renamed places that already had been inhabited and named for countless generations. But to the European mind, it was all new. Thus we have "New France," "New Amsterdam," "New England," "New Spain," and, overall, the "New World," with the names of European cities, nations, and individuals imposed upon the land.

The Indian people were also renamed as individuals, a process that began in the sixteenth century and continued into the twentieth. For five hundred years, the common practice has been that whenever an Indian is converted to Christianity, that man or woman has to be renamed, baptized with a "real" Christian name. Here, in brief, is one of the earliest documented stories of such renaming (*The Spanish Jesuit Mission in Virginia* by Clifford Lewis and Albert Loomier, University of North Carolina Press, 1953).

Around 1560 a Powhatan youth was "picked up" (that is, kidnapped) by a party of Spaniards off the coast of what would become known as Virginia. Taken to Mexico, he was baptized by the Jesuits with the name of his abductor, Don Luis de Velasco. From there, the new Don Luis was shipped to Havana to be further prepared for his new role as a guide and interpreter for Spanish colonizers. Ten years passed before he returned to his homeland on September 10, 1570, guiding a small group of Jesuit priests. To the Spaniards' dismay, Don Luis was more interested in reuniting with his people and returning to his "heathen ways" (which including resuming a leadership role among his people and getting married) than being their interpreter. He lived with the priests "but two nights before going back to his village." There he remained, ignoring the Jesuits' demands that he come back to them. Months passed, and the priests became so insistent in demanding the return of their apostate convert that the Powhatans apparently lost patience with the troublesome Coatmen and wiped all of them out, with the exception of a young Spanish boy, who was likely judged to be blameless. Don Luis, whose Indian name was never recorded, was sought by the

Spanish in a punitive expedition in 1572. However, though they recovered the Spanish boy, Alonso (who told them that their former interpreter was still living), they never managed to recapture Don Luis.

I have two renaming stories to share from more recent times. The first was recounted to me by a Nez Perce friend, Phil George, whose grandfather was told by an Indian agent that he would have to accept a "real" name. In those days, it was common for agents to choose a name such as that of a president to replace a person's original name. But Phil's grandfather had his own ideas about names.

a lover of horses

"You," the Indian agent said to my grandfather, *"will now be 'George Washington.'"*

My grandfather was not ignorant about American history. He knew the meaning of that name. There was no way that he would accept it. However, he had a suggestion. Our Nez Perce people have a great love for horses. We gained a reputation as being among the finest horse breeders in the world when we developed the breed now called the Appaloosa. My grandfather had learned that the name "Phillip" literally means "lover of horses."

"I will use George as my last name," my grandfather said. *"I will be Phillip George."*

I first met Louis Littlecoon Oliver when he was in his seventies and he came to a workshop that several other Native authors and I were doing at Flaming Rainbow College in Oklahoma. A native of Tahlequah, Louis was an incredible storehouse of knowledge. Not only did he know his own Creek language and traditions, but he was one of the last Yuchi speakers and often called upon by the

Cherokees to help them with the revival of their stomp dances. Although he had never published anything before other than letters in newspapers, Louis was so inspired by meeting young Indian writers—and so incredibly creative—that he quickly progressed from writing imitations of Victorian verse to powerful modern poems and short stories. By the time of his passing fifteen years later, four books of his stories and poems had been published, his work had been translated into a dozen different languages, and he had been named Writer of the Year in Oklahoma.

Any time that you spent with Louis was always full of surprises. You never knew what he would show you or tell you that would move you to laughter or tears or to just plain awe about how much this little old man with a grandfatherly face knew and had done in his lifetime. One day, when I was visiting Louis, he leaned over and said, "Joe, I ever tell you how I got my name?"

"Tell me," I said.

name allotment

Well, when it came time for allotment, everybody had to go down and report to the Indian agent to get their land. When my mother went to get my father, he was drunk. That made her mad. She just picked me up, I was only a baby then, and went along without him. But when she got down to the office, it turned out that the Indian agent was drunk, too, and so was the man who was his interpreter. So when it came my mother's turn, she was just a-hoppin' mad.

"What's your name?" the Indian agent asked.

"Don't got no name," my mother answered.

The Indian agent turned to the interpreter for some help. Well, he recognized my mother and he said, "That there is Hattie Tiger."

"Hattie Tiger, is that your name?" the agent said.

"Don't got no name," my mother said again. She was that mad.

"Well, what's your baby's name, then?"

"He's got no name."

By then, the Indian agent had about had it.

"In that case, then, I'm going to give him a name. He can have my name. Louis Oliver."

And that's what he wrote down, and that's how I came to be named after a drunk Indian agent.

Indians with European names. Nez Perce is, of course, not the name that Phil's people call themselves in their own language. Nor did Louis Oliver's ancestors call themselves Creeks. Nez Perce means "Pierced Nose" in French, emanating from the practice among some of the Indian nations of the Great Basin of piercing their noses and wearing ornaments in them. (Interestingly enough, the practice was apparently less common among the Nez Perce than certain other tribes.) The Nez Perce call themselves Nimipoom, which means "The People." The Creek people, who call themselves Muskogee, were named "Creek" because of all of the rivers found in their original homelands in what is now Alabama and Mississippi. When European explorers first encountered them, they were an alliance of more than fifty towns that spoke six distinct languages, the most common of which was Muskogee.

It is rather amazing how many of the contemporary names applied to Indian nations by the United States government and the general public come from European languages or the tribal languages of other Native nations that were often their enemies. It is not an exaggeration to say that this is true of almost every well-known American Indian tribal nation. Following is a brief list of some of the best-known aboriginal peoples of North America who were renamed after the coming of Europeans. In each case, the new name is followed by the original Native name and its meaning.

Abenaki: Alnobak, "The People"

Apache: Tinneh, "The People"

Arapaho: Hinaneina, "The People"

Cherokee: Aniyunwiya, "The Principal People"

Cheyenne: Tsit-tsit-sas, "Striped Arrow People"

Chippewa (or Ojibway): Anishinabe, "Real People"

Creek: Muskogee (The Muskogee were a confederacy of many towns, and the exact meaning of the word is now uncertain.)

Crow: Absaroke, "Bird People"

Delaware: Lenape, "Real People"

Eskimo: Inuit or Inupiat, "The People"

Fox (or Sauk and Fox): Mesquakie, "Red Earth People"

Huron: Wendat, "Island People"

Iroquois: Haudenosaunee, "People of the Longhouse," or Ongwe-Onweh, "Real People"

Navajo: Diné, "The People"

Nez Perce: Nimipoom, "The People"

Seminole: means "Those who have run away from the towns" in Muskogee, people of the lower Creek nations who sought refuge and resisted the U.S. Army in the Florida swamps.

Sioux: Lakota (or Dakota or Nakota—there are three separate dialects), "Allies"

Shoshone: Numi, "The People"

Winnebago: Ho-Chunk, "People of the Big Speech"

i would have joined the apaches

As much as European colonists, explorers, missionaries, and soldiers contested with American Indians for control of the continent, it also seems that, from the first European contact, virtually every non-Native person who spent any time with American Indians was moved and changed by the experience. Despite blinding prejudice, innumerable misunderstandings occasioned by differences in language and culture, greed that elevated gold above human souls, and what now seems to be a pervasive obtuseness on the part of every government agency ever entrusted with Indian affairs, the greatest praise of the Native people of the continent has, for centuries, come from white people themselves—including men whose job it was to face them in battle. Indeed, there is a deep note of regret and even personal recrimination in many of their writings. In *The Gospel of the Redman*, Ernest Thompson Seton records these words spoken to him in 1935 by Neil Erickson, a white scout who fought in the Army campaigns against Geronimo and Victorio: "If I had known then what I know now about Indian character, I would have deserted from the American army and joined up with the Apaches."

This sympathy for the Indians' plight became evident in certain writers of the nineteenth century who attempted to accurately portray the lives and true character of American Indians. The artist George Catlin was one of those. Not only in his superb canvases, but in his popular lectures and such books as *Manners, Customs and Conditions of the North American Indians* (1841), Catlin labored to paint true pictures of Native people. Catlin's monumental work includes this quote from Christopher Columbus, writing to the King and Queen of Spain about his first voyage to Hispaniola: "I swear to your Majesties that there is not a better people in the world than these; more affectionate, affable, or mild. They love their neighbors as themselves, and they always speak smilingly."

Sadly, Columbus's feelings about the Indians of Hispaniola changed. In his later writings he portrayed them as fierce and cannibalistic. Perhaps his ruthless quest for gold and power led him to try to justify his actions. The islands of the West Indies were depopulated within twenty years of his arrival, with perhaps as many as 500,000 Indians wiped out. Most of them were the victims of Spanish oppression—forced into mines to dig for the gold that was more precious to Europeans than human lives. Columbus is one of the first who began the long process of hiding the true face of the Indian. That European-imposed mask—half monster, half noble savage—would remain on the face of American Indians for another four centuries.

a white man and an indian

Some of the growing public awareness of the real face of the American Indian may be traced to the administration of President Ulysses S. Grant, though before his untimely death, Abraham Lincoln did say, "If I live, this accursed system of robbery and shame in our treatment of Indians shall be reformed." Grant was the first president to place an American Indian in a position of national authority when he named Ely S. Parker, a Seneca, to be Commissioner of Indian Affairs. Parker's own story is as interesting as Grant's (actually Parker's) Peace Policy, the first ever proclaimed by the United States government.

But the peace policy and Parker's tenure would be brief. Parker served as Commissioner of Indian Affairs only from April 26, 1869 to August 1, 1871. After only two years, his career in government ended when he resigned following a congressional inquiry into his purported misdeeds. That inquiry—which actually found him not guilty—was propelled by powerful business interests who had discovered that Parker's honesty prevented them from defrauding the government and cheating the Indians. (Among other things, with a smile on his face as he did so, Parker replaced corrupt Indian agents with Quakers.) Parker's downfall shows, I suppose, how much things have changed and still remain the same in Washington, D.C. Military contracts in the late eighteenth century were as important then as they are now. Rather than selling new weapons systems, though, one of the most lucrative endeavors was that of providing the supplies promised under treaty to the western Indians. Before Parker took office, however, there was so much corruption that it was not uncommon for a herd of cattle to be delivered to a reservation, where the agent would collect his payment. Then, before a single Indian could be fed, that same herd would be driven off to be sold by the original suppliers to another reservation down the line, while the white Indian agent pocketed a hefty bribe. When the starving Indians were finally given meat and grain, the meat was often rotten and the grain moldy.

The consequences of such cheating were often grave. Not only did it result in Indians starving, but it led to major uprisings. The Santee Sioux 1862 Minnesota Outbreak, which occurred seven years before Parker took office, is a case in point. Not only did the traders refuse to give the promised stores to the starving Santees, but one trader, Andrew Myrick, told the hungry Sioux, "Go and eat grass." Under the reluctant leadership of Little Crow, the Santees finally could take no more. They fought their way into the warehouses, killing twenty men, and then took on a company of forty-five soldiers, of whom only twenty-four escaped. Before they were defeated by superior white forces, the Santees attacked the town of New Ulm, burning half of it to the ground, and laid siege to Fort Ridgely. Dozens of people died and thirty-eight Santees were hanged on December 26 in Mankato in the largest public execution in American history.

None of this would have happened had the Sioux simply been fed. The epic tragedy of the Northern Cheyenne exodus from Indian Territory led by Little Wolf and Dull Knife in 1878 (seven years after Parker left office) was also a direct result of similar official ineptitude and neglect. Their heroic attempt to return to their Montana homelands resulted in the deaths of nearly half their number.

Ely Parker was aware of the corruption of the "Indian Ring." More than perhaps any other American of his generation, white or Indian, he knew the ways of the world. There have been few men in American history as interesting as he. His Iroquois name, Donehogawa, indicated his position as a traditional chief of his people, the "Grand Sachem," or principal chief, of the Iroquois, yet his background had been a unique mixture of Iroquois tradition and white education. The Iroquois had tried to remain neutral during the American Revolution. However, some Iroquois, especially Mohawks and Senecas, had chosen to fight for the British, while others, in particular the Oneidas and Tuscaroras, supported the cause of the colonists. In fact, had not the Oneidas and Tuscaroras donated tons of food, carried on their backs to the troops of George Washington when the American armies were starving at Valley Forge, the American conflict might have had a very different ending. The treaties and land cessions that followed the Revolution were brutal to the Iroquois. One of the results was that certain farsighted Iroquois leaders decided the only way to fight the whites was not with guns, but with their own ways. Some of their own children would have to be educated as whites to fight better for their people. One of the children chosen was a boy whose name was then Hasanoanda, which might be translated as "The Reader," the young Ely Parker. They could not have made a better choice. He came from a distinguished family. His mother was *ho-ya-neh,* one of the women who chose the chiefs and a direct descendant of Handsome Lake, the Iroquois prophet and the famous Seneca Chief Cornplanter. Her great-uncle, who visited their home and told stories to young Ely, was none other than Red Jacket.

Though he faced prejudice and hardship, young Ely succeeded so admirably at the start of his education that he went on to Yates Academy. After meeting Lewis Henry Morgan in Albany, he became Morgan's primary informant for the groundbreaking volume *League of the Ho-de-no-sau-nee or Iroquois,* published in 1851, the first scientific account of an American Indian people. In fact, the book is dedicated to "Ha-sa-no-an-da" (Ely S. Parker), a Seneca Indian, this work, the materials of which are the fruit of our joint researches." Financial support from Morgan and his friends enabled Parker to continue his education and attend Cayuga Academy. He began traveling to Albany and Washington while in his teens to interpret and speak for Seneca land claims. Before he reached the age of twenty he had become fluent not only in English, but also Greek and Latin, while gaining the training that he hoped would qualify him to be a lawyer. A magnificent public speaker, he had already met and been entertained by every governor of New York and two presidents, Polk and Taylor. (He would also go on to have warm relations and even personal friendships with every one of the next five American presidents.) Largely through his efforts, the Seneca claims to their reservation at Tonawanda (which remains in Seneca hands to this day) were successful, and Parker was elevated in 1851 by the Clan Mothers to the Grand Sachemship that carried the name Donehogawa, which means "Open Door." He was only twenty-three years old.

Parker would go on to become a civil engineer in Galena, Illinois, where he met the man who would become a close friend, Ulysses S. Grant. During the Civil War, he served as Grant's personal secretary, with the rank of Brevet General, and became part of Grant's administration, when he was appointed Commissioner of Indian Affairs.

Throughout his life, Parker excelled in both the white and Indian worlds, despite numerous setbacks. The path of the white man chosen for him by his elders had propelled him to fame and enabled him to help his people. Although Parker chose to live most of his adult life away from his Seneca people, married a white woman, and lived in Connecticut, he never turned his back on his people's traditions nor viewed them with scorn. Ironically, a much harsher and more demeaning version of that white man's road that Parker had followed would be the forced lot of generations of American Indian young people after him with the birth of government-run Indian boarding schools whose motto would be "Kill the Indian and save the man."

contact: the coming of europeans

Recommended Reading

Cook-Lynn, Elizabeth (Dakota). *Aurelia: A Crow Creek Trilogy.* Denver: University Press of
    Colorado, 1999. This epic novel tells of a Native nation facing Euro-American
    colonialism and its consequences.

Matthews, John Joseph (Osage). *Wah'Kon-Tah: The Osage and the White Man's Road.*
    Norman: University of Oklahoma Press, 1932. This novel explores the complicated
    relationship between the Osage Nation and a sympathetic Indian agent.

Parker, Arthur C. (Seneca). *Red Jacket: Seneca Chief* (originally published in 1956).
    Lincoln: University of Nebraska Press, 1998. This biography of the Seneca orator and
    leader was written by his great-nephew.

Welch, James (Blackfeet). *Fools Crow.* New York: Penguin, 1986. This magnificent
    historical novel focuses on the Blackfeet nation in the late 1800s at a time when a
    young Blackfeet warrior's lie about a dream vision and the coming of the whites
    disrupt traditional life.

———. *Killing Custer.* New York: Penguin, 1995. Welch presents a modern non-fiction
    reconsideration of the Little Bighorn battle from the Indian viewpoint.

corn

On the Tecolote fields
the corn is growing green.
I came there, I saw the tassels
waving in the breeze
and I whistled softly for joy.

—Tohono O'odham corn song

Corn, the One Who Sustains Life, gave herself to our people. In the Abenaki story of the origin of corn, there was a time when the people were starving. Then a woman dressed in green, a woman with flowing yellow hair, appeared to a hunter.

"I have come to help your people," she said. "I have come to sacrifice myself so that your people can live. I am going to die now. Loosen the earth in this clearing and then drag my body across it. Keep my grave free of weeds and you will see me again."

It happened just as the Corn Maiden said. She fell to the earth without breath. Her body grew smaller and smaller as the man dragged her across the earth, and then she was gone. He kept watch on the clearing, pulling out the weeds and driving away the birds and animals that would have disturbed her grave. Small shoots, as green as her clothing, grew up from the earth, and as they grew to the height of a person, tassels as golden as the Corn Maiden's hair appeared on top of each plant, followed by the first ears of corn upon each stalk. So it was that Corn gave herself to help feed the people.

There are innumerable tales of the origin of corn, virtually one for every Indian nation that relied upon corn. Indian corn is so important to the Iroquois people that it is called *onenhah,* "the life sustainer." It is also referred to by the Iroquois (with squash and beans) as one of the "Three Sisters." (Beans provide nitrogen for the soil, and the corn provides a support for the beans to twine upon, while the wide umbrella leaves of the squash shade out weeds and keep in moisture.) The origin stories of the Mayan peoples of Central America explain that they are "Men of Maize." The first real humans, they explain, were made from ears of corn. Maize, whose name may have been derived from the Arawak language of the Caribbean, is a sacred plant in virtually all American Indian cultures. The Pueblo author Alfonso Ortiz described corn as being "Mother, Enabler, Transformer and Healer." Throughout the Americas, corn is viewed not as just a food, but as a benevolent being to be thanked in ceremony and cherished as one would cherish a beloved elder.

Corn and people are truly interdependent. Corn is not a wild plant, but a crop that was developed by the Native agronomists of the American continents over the course of thousands of years. Without the aid of human beings, corn cannot successfully reseed itself, but dies out within a few years. We must save the corn for it to save us. By the time Europeans arrived in the Americas, there were at least 150 varieties of corn being grown from southern Chile to Canada. The Three Sisters complex of the Northeast, which appears to have been in place for at least eight hundred years, is only one example of the many sophisticated systems of corn growing and corn varieties developed, making it possible to raise corn in deserts, rain forests, river valleys, and on high mountain slopes.

No food crop in the world is of more cultural, economic, and spiritual importance than corn. Exported from the Americas in the sixteenth century, it rapidly became one of the world's more important cash crops. It might be said, despite the mountains of precious metal stolen by the conquistadors from the Native peoples of Peru and Mexico, that maize was the true gold of the New World. The yearly cash value of corn crops worldwide in 1989 was estimated by Arturo Warman, a professor at Universidad Autoctona de Mexico, to be more than 200 billion dollars.

Ironically, because of corn's incredibly high yields, portability (dried kernels of corn are one of the easiest and most efficient of foods to transport), and high nutritive value, its introduction to Africa made the slave trade more possible. African populations grew larger with the introduction of corn. Unlike wheat, corn prevents the vitamin deficiency condition known as scurvy and was used to feed slaves as they were transported to the Americas.

More than any other plant, corn comes closest to being both the perfect food and the perfect crop. No other cereal grain has a higher yield. What is yield? If you plant one seed of a cereal and harvest six seeds, the yield is 6:1. This was the standard European yield for wheat. (Wheat, it should be explained, was called "corn" long before the introduction to Europe of *Zea mays,* Indian corn. The word "corn" simply means a hard grain or a seed. So, even though there are references to corn as a food crop in Europe long before the fifteenth century, they are not talking about Indian corn.) The average yield for corn in the New World at the time of European arrival was more than 100:1. In some places, the yield was as much as 800:1, which is an astronomical difference. It is clear, considering crop yields alone, why Indian corn was adopted so quickly and enthusiastically in Europe, Africa, and Asia that by the seventeenth century many people thought Indian corn had its origin in Europe or Asia, where it was often called "Turkish corn."

Yet there is no doubt that corn first came from the American continents. Sustainer and faithful friend, no plant is more beloved to American Indians than Mother Corn, our great gift to the world.

generations: parents, grandparents, children

GRANDMOTHER FILLED A PLACE THAT MOTHER DID NOT FILL,

AND THE OLDER SHE GOT, IT SEEMED, THE MORE WE CHILDREN

DEPENDED UPON HER FOR ATTENTION.

—*Luther Standing Bear (Lakota), 1931*

gluskonba's grandmother

(ABENAKI)

Here is where my story camps. It is long ago, not long after Gluskonba has shaped himself from the dust that falls from the hands of Ktsi Nwaskw. Because Gluskonba has great power but knows almost nothing, Ktsi Nwaskw sees that he needs someone to guide him. So Ktsi Nwaskw gives Gluskonba a grandmother. Woodchuck, who is wise and knows many things, Woodchuck who digs deep into the earth and sees

what is beneath things, Woodchuck becomes the grandmother of Gluskonba.
Whenever Gluskonba does something foolish, it is always Grandmother who points
out the error of his ways.

One day Gluskonba decides to go fishing. He goes down to the river to fish, but
all the fish see him coming. They know what he has in mind.

Perhaps it is because, as he approaches the river, Gluskonba chants loudly:

I am going fishing,
I will catch many fish and eat them.
I am going fishing,
I will catch many fish and eat them.

But, because the fish all swam away, there are no fish to be caught. When he
realizes that he is not going to catch any fish, Gluskonba is not happy. He goes
straight home to Grandmother's lodge.

"Grandmother," he says, "make a fish trap for me."

"Why do you want me to do this?" Grandmother Woodchuck asks.

At that, Gluskonba sits down. Then Gluskonba begins to chant:

Make a fish trap for me,
Make a fish trap for me,
Make a fish trap for me,
Make a fish trap for me.

Grandmother Woodchuck covers her ears. "Grandson," she says, "Stop your
chanting. You are giving me a headache. I know how stubborn you are and that you
will keep asking until I do as you ask. So I will make a fish trap for you."

Then Grandmother Woodchuck weaves Gluskonba a strong fish trap.

"Wliwini, Nokomis," Gluskonba says. "Thank you, Grandmother."

Because Grandmother has made this fish trap, this fish trap has great power; Gluskonba sees this. This fish trap may seem small, but it can stretch to hold all that swim into it. Straight to the river Gluskonba goes.

Seeing him coming, hearing his feet strike the ground, the fish swim away and hide beneath the stones. Gluskonba pays them no mind; he sits beside the river and he weeps. Loudly this Gluskonba weeps.

"All the fish will die," he sobs. "Surely this will happen."

Hearing his words, the fish come out from their hiding places; they swim close to him.

"Gluskonba," the fish say, "why will we die?"

Gluskonba looks at the fish. He shakes his head. "It is sad to tell. All the waters will dry up and so you will die."

The fish are frightened. "What can we do?" they say.

Gluskonba smiles. "You can swim into my fish trap. This trap will hold the water and you will be able to survive."

He puts his trap into the river. All of the fish in the river swim into the trap and are caught. He is happy, this Gluskonba. He calls Grandmother to see what he has done.

"Nokomis," Gluskonba says, "see this. It is a good thing. Now it will be easy to catch fish. All we need to do is reach into my trap and pull them out. You see, I have all the fish in the river."

But Grandmother Woodchuck shakes her head. "It is not good, grandson," she says. "If you keep all the fish in a trap, they will eventually die in there. Then there will be none for the future, for our children to come. One person cannot own all the fish."

Gluskonba hears her words. "Nokomis," he says, "I see that you are right." So he opens his fish trap and releases the fish. So it is that since then, no fish trap has ever been able to catch all the fish.

half a blanket

(MOHAWK)

Long ago, there was a time when game became scarce and life was not easy for the people. In one longhouse, there was an old man who had grown so weak that he could scarcely walk. His eyesight and his memory were failing, and now it was difficult for him to do anything to help his family.

Finally, one day, the old man's son, who saw how much his family had to do to care for his elderly father, grew impatient. "It is not right," he thought, "that we should have to share our food with my father when we have barely enough to feed ourselves. It is time for him to go into the forest."

So the man called his own eldest son to him. He picked up a deerskin blanket and handed it to the boy.

"My son," he said, "I am sorry to say this, but we can no longer take care of your grandfather. You must take him into the forest far from our longhouse and abandon him there. It is the only thing we can do. You can wrap this blanket around his shoulders so that he will at least have some final comfort."

The boy looked hard at his father, but he said nothing. He took the blanket. Then he helped his grandfather to his feet and guided him deep into the forest until he came to a big tree that had soft moss around its base. He helped his grandfather sit down under the tree.

"You will be comfortable here, Grandfather," the grandson said. Then the boy took out his knife, cut the deerskin blanket exactly in half, and carried the other half back to the longhouse.

As soon as the boy walked in, his father spoke to him.

"Did you take your grandfather far into the forest as I asked?" the father said.

"I did," the son answered.

"Why did you bring back half of the blanket?" asked the father.

generations: parents, grandparents, children

*"My father," said the boy, "when you grow old and there is nothing more that we
can do, I will wrap this blanket around your shoulders after I abandon you in the forest."*

*"Ah," said the man. Then he was silent for a long time. Finally he looked up at
his son. "Go into the forest and bring back your grandfather."*

The image of life as a circle has many meanings. Imagine it as a circle divided
into the four stages of life. We begin that journey as a newborn child and continue
around the circle from childhood into youth and then into adulthood. Finally, if
we are fortunate enough to enjoy long life, we become elders. And the place of
the elder on the circle approaches that of the child. In many American Indian
nations, the elders and children are both seen as sacred. The world is new in the
eyes of every child, as bright and shining as the first dew on the spring grasses. For
the elder, the world is similarly understood in the eyes of memory. Both the child
and the elder are closer to the Creator than the generations in between them.

The circle teaches us that elders and children were always meant to be close
to each other. It is no accident that, in every part of the world, we often see that
there is a special understanding and bond between children and their grandparents.
Universally human as this may be, there are many aspects of Western culture that
have created a deep gulf, physically and culturally, between the old and the young.
American Indians sometimes view the absence of elders in the average American
family as one of the reasons why there is so much trouble in this world. Nowhere
are elders more cherished or children more loved than in American Indian
communities, especially those most in touch with their traditions.

One striking image of the relationship between the generations was given me
by my friend Oren Lyons. As an Onondaga Faithkeeper and one who speaks for
peace in what has now become a time-honored Iroquois tradition, Oren has traveled
throughout the United States and in many nations, from the former Soviet Union

and Bosnia to Brazil and nations in the South Pacific. His mission is to share with all human beings those much-needed teachings of reconciliation, forgiveness, and the transformation of grief into positive action that were given to the People of the Longhouse countless generations ago, when a messenger called the Peacemaker was sent by the Creator to lead the warring Iroquois nations into a Great League of Peace. With Hiawatha by his side, the Peacemaker took the teachings of that Great Law to the Senecas, the Cayugas, the Oneidas, the Mohawks, and the Onondagas, who embraced them all. At Onondaga a hole was dug in the earth and the war club symbolically buried under the roots of a great pine tree.

That mission of spreading the Haudenosaunee word of peace is one shared by a number of contemporary Iroquois. There is, for example, Jake Swamp, a Mohawk subchief who has founded the Tree of Peace Society. Like Oren, Jake travels the globe. He tells the story of the Great League of Peace and then plants trees of peace on which are hung white, yellow, black, and red ribbons symbolizing the four colors of humanity. Like Oren Lyons, Jake Swamp takes seriously that role of the elder in caring for the people and thinking of the generations to come. It is commonly said among not only the Iroquois (who may have originated this concept—or maybe not) that we need to always consider Seven Generations. When we take any action, we must ask ourselves what the consequences of that deed will be—not tomorrow, not four years from now, but seven generations in the future.

One winter at Onondaga I shared the stage with Oren in a small storytelling festival held at the Onondaga Nation School. The audience was made up of Onondaga children, their parents, and their teachers. All of the generations were there, and Oren chose to tell a story about something that had happened to him. The previous summer he had been invited to the reservation of one of the Northern Plains nations for their Sun dance. Some of the details he shared in his story I know were meant only for that audience at Onondaga, and so I won't relate them or be specific about what reservation he was visiting. But the part

that Oren told me could be shared, should be shared, with all people is this:
There were different-color poles over each of the arbors around the Sun dance
grounds. An old man of that Plains nation asked Oren a question. Because Oren
gave him the right answer, the elder then chose to explain to Oren the significance
of those poles, which stood for the different generations, the different stages of a
person's life. Here, in my own words, is how I heard and how I have grown to
understand those stages:

the lesson of the sun dance poles

The first stands for that part of your life from birth until about the age of twenty.
During those years you are a Child. As a child, it is your duty to listen, to grow
physically, to make mistakes, but to learn from those mistakes. Not only the
parents, but also everyone in the community has some responsibility in caring for
the child.

The second represents that period from twenty to thirty. During those years you
are a Child With Children. Although you are old enough and physically prepared to
have children of your own, there is still much that you have to learn and many ways
you must grow in mind and spirit and emotion. You must turn to others, especially
your own parents and relatives, to assist you in raising your children. At this time in
your life you learn to care for others and place their needs before your own. These
are also physically strong years in which, as a warrior, as a hunter, as one who grows
crops or gathers food, you protect and provide for your family.

The third is the years from thirty to forty. In those years you finally become an
Adult. You begin to take on responsibilities beyond those of your family, community
responsibilities. Those skills that you have been given—and each person has his or
her own special skills—grow during those years, and others may begin to turn to you

for help and guidance, and in certain ways you may take on small roles of leadership. It may be your job to carry messages to other nations and travel.

The fourth stands for the time between your fortieth and fiftieth years. Not all people will reach this age, so there are fewer of you. You may remain strong, but your body has changed: your shoulders and hips and waist have broadened from the years and the loads you have borne. Your children now have children of their own, and you have become a Grandparent. You may be a good teacher for your grandchildren because this is the second time that you have seen it all happen and your memory has held what you learned. This is the time when men may take on the roles of Chiefs and women may become Clan Mothers and leaders of the women's societies. When you speak, you speak for the people.

The fifth symbolizes the period from fifty to sixty. If you are one of the leaders of the men or the women, now is the time when you may be chosen to head their councils. If you are an artist of some kind, this may be when your work reaches its peak and others come to you for you to teach them. Because you have lived as long as you have, your stories have grown very strong, even though your body may now be weakening. The first flecks of snow may be seen in your hair, each white hair the sign of something you have learned that the people will need to remember.

The sixth is those years from sixty to seventy. Your job now is that of the Elder and maybe that of the Great-Grandparent. The snows of many seasons rest on your head, and those who see you, see your white hair as a gift from the Creator, as a badge of honor, like the white head of the eagle. It is a special honor that the Creator has allowed you to live all these years, for many do not survive the hardships that are part of every human life. You are the one who teaches the teachers.

The seventh stands for that period of your life from seventy to eighty. You have become treasured by your people. You no longer travel much, but those who wish to learn now come to you. They listen and they learn from your words and from your presence. It is a time when you may continue to work and do those things that you have now learned so well, care for those you love and for all the people. But it is also a time when you can rest and watch, take pleasure in the lives around you, in seeing the good that you have shared become part of the strength of your people. Your walk along the circle is almost done and you look around you at times as if looking down from the great height of a mountain.

The eighth is for those years after eighty, for as many or as few as there are. Because you are so precious, have learned and shared so much, each of those years, each winter that you survive, is a special gift from the Creator—not to you, but to your people, who are able to have you remain with them. Some people who live this long go so far around the circle that they become a child again. They forget the things they learned, the losses they suffered, and they are as simple and carefree as a child. Now their children and their children's children must care for them, for the old one has become as weak as a baby, has no teeth, cannot stand. This second childhood is also a gift from the Great Mystery, a gift to you who have been given this freeing of your mind, a gift to your family who have been given a chance to give back some small part of the care they received from you throughout your long life.

Though it may not always be that way, that is the way our Creator meant it to be for our generations.

Indeed, it is true, tragically so, that all too many American Indians find it hard to live that path. They suffer from many of the same social problems with their elders and their children that trouble the average American. The difficulties of maintaining an American lifestyle, holding down a demanding job and providing a place for elders in your lives, caring for your elders when they can no longer take care of themselves, and making it possible for grandparents to be with grandchildren, are now issues in American Indian communities, too. Problems with drug abuse, despair, suicide (suicide rates among American Indian children are the highest of any group in the United States), teenage pregnancy, and gang violence have become awful realities for not only urban Indian populations but those still living on reservations in every part the country.

Yet there are many American Indians who know just how recent these problems are for our people. They also have a very clear idea of what began this slide into difficulty and despair.

Warm Springs Millennium: Voices from the Reservation, by Michael Baughman and Charlotte Hadella, focuses on the Warm Springs Reservation in Oregon. Extended interviews and information about the community's history give an intimate portrait of the lives of the 3,600 Paiute, Wascos, and Warm Springs Indians who make it their home. One of the most poignant stories told in the book is about the 1997 vandalizing of the tribe's culture and heritage center, in which computers were smashed and the disks containing Native language archives and stories from now-departed elders were smashed. Saddest of all, the two twelve-year-olds who did it were Indian kids themselves. Like many Native communities, Warm Springs has been dealing with teenage gangs and children who feel such frustration that they just feel the need to destroy something. Wilson Wewa, Jr., a Northern Paiute and director of the Warm Springs Culture and Heritage Center, saw it as a result of that break in the circle of culture that has affected so many Native communities. He talked not with anger, but with regret about what the children had done. It was only one sign of a problem that had begun a century ago when the United States government instituted government boarding schools. As a result of separating children from other generations in their communities, today there are parents and grandparents who do not know how to play their traditional roles or who are not given the opportunity because their lives have become almost as fragmented (or, as they put it, as selfish) as those of the non-Indians in the communities around them.

What is the answer? As with all of the great questions of our time—questions that touch both Indian and non-Indian alike—there is never just one answer. But there are places we can look to begin to learn. When I ask this of the elders who have taught me, they point back to the circle. What we need is to return in some way to that old way. Not literally back to the wigwam and the tipi, the hunting of the deer and the buffalo, to a world with no cars or paved roads, no automobiles or airplanes, no multinational corporations that swallow people as greedily as the Sucking Monsters of our old tales devoured the human beings (Ah, but can you guess what happened when that Sucking Monster swallowed Coyote? Too bad for that monster!); but simply back to the heart of memory. In that way, we may find again the old ways to survive. We may recognize the truths of our old stories and then each change our world by acting upon them. Stories are a circle of dreams. In dreams, all things are possible.

Recommended Reading

Baughman, Michael, and Hadella, Charlotte. *Warm Springs Millennium: Voices from the Reservation*. Austin: University of Texas Press, 2000. This collection of personal narratives is a unique reflection of contemporary reservation life.

Erdrich, Louise (Chippewa). *Love Medicine*. New York: Holt, 1984. One of the most highly praised and powerful intergenerational novels of the last twenty years, Erdrich's book spans two centuries and five generations of Indian family life.

Fawcett (Tantaquidgeon), Melissa Jayne (Mohegan). *Medicine Trail*. Tucson: University of Arizona Press, 2001. Fawcett tells the inspiring story of her aunt, Gladys Tantaquidgeon, a Mohegan medicine woman, ethnologist, and elder whose life spans more than one hundred years.

Red Shirt, Delphine (Lakota). *Bead on an Anthill: a Lakota Childhood*. Lincoln: University of Nebraska Press, 1998. This poignant, spiritual memoir describes growing up on the Pine Ridge Reservation in the 1960s and 1970s.

indian boarding schools

Minnewa Ka, Kah Wah We!
Minnewa Ka, Kah Wah We!
Minnewa Ka, Kah Wah We!
Carlisle! Carlisle! Carlisle!

—*Carlisle Indian School song chanted by*
   student fans at Carlisle football games, circa 1908

Twenty years ago, my friend Swift Eagle told me the story of how he ended up in an Indian boarding school. His Apache grandfather had gone with him up into the hills to keep him from being taken. So, while other boys were dragged off to the boarding school, Swift Eagle was living off the land in the old way with his grandfather. However, the U.S. Army was sent to bring in the Indian children who had escaped them, and Swift Eagle was caught. They brought him down to the railhead, where he was put into a group of other young people waiting for the arrival of the train. People were looking at him, even the other Indians, for he was bare-chested and wearing a big shell pendant. This was the early 1900s, and most of the Pueblos and Apaches in New Mexico were not dressing that way anymore.

"I really looked like a wild Indian," he chuckled.

Then, he said, "I heard an awful scream, like the howling of some terrible monster. 'It is coming,' people were saying. 'It is coming.' They were pointing along these two long, long pieces of metal that were laid on the ground. Then the ground started to shake, and those long, shiny pieces of metal began to shiver. I looked where everyone was pointing and I saw this huge creature coming. It looked like a giant tomato worm, and there was smoke coming out of it. That monster was coming right toward us. I looked around—everyone was just standing there, and I thought they were too frightened to move. 'Come on,' I shouted in our language, 'follow me. I'll lead you to safety. Let's get away from that monster.' Then I started to run, but no one followed me except two of the army men, who tackled me and then put me in leg irons so I couldn't run away. They picked me up and carried me right up into that monster, the first train I had ever seen. That was how I ended up going off to Indian boarding school in chains."

Indian boarding schools. Everybody who ended up in one and survived had more than one story about his or her experiences. Founded in 1879 by Lieutenant Richard Henry Pratt and sited in an abandoned army barracks in Carlisle, Pennsylvania, the Carlisle Indian School was the first and most famous of these military-style institutions. There, Indian boys had their hair cut and were dressed in uniforms, and girls were outfitted with loose Mother Hubbard dresses. Both sexes were subjected to discipline in every sense of that word, from the morning bugle at six to evening taps at nine. Carlisle's first class numbered 147. By 1917, the enrollment was more than seven hundred and included more than fifty tribes.

Lieutenant Pratt was a veteran of the 10th Cavalry, the famous Buffalo Soldiers, a black regiment with white officers. From what he had learned from his African-American men and his Indian scouts, Pratt developed a respect for minorities and a desire to help them "better" themselves. The humanitarian mission of Carlisle was to prepare Indians for assimilation as equals into American culture. That the Indians had no say in the matter was, to Pratt, a necessity. As Pratt said in an address to the United States Congress, "We accept the watchword; let us by patient effort kill the Indian in him and save the man." Not just children were sent to Carlisle. Among Pratt's students were men in their twenties and thirties who had ridden to war against the army, now reduced to the status of stiff-uniformed students in the dormitory barracks of Carlisle.

The success of Pratt's Carlisle experiment led to the founding of numerous other similar boarding schools throughout the continent. By 1897, more than fourteen thousand American Indians were in twenty-seven boarding schools, but the mission of those schools was about to change. A new generation of bureaucrats, such as Estelle Reel, the superintendent of Indian boarding schools from 1898 to 1910, was much less optimistic than Pratt. Indians were racially inferior and suffered, according to Reel, from "unfortunate heredity." The best that could be done would be to train them to be laborers in the trades and servants in the home, and the limited curricula of the schools would reflect that low expectation.

Rather than finding an education, a great many Indian children discovered other things—both tragic and otherwise—at Indian schools. Many of them tried to run away, walking hundreds of miles back to the homes and families and lands where they had left their hearts. Every boarding school has stories of kids who were killed by trains while walking home along the tracks or who died from exposure. Not that there was any shortage of mortality at the schools themselves. If you walk, as I have walked, in the graveyards behind any of those schools, such as the Haskell Institute in Kansas (now an American Indian college), you will see headstones carved with the names of young men and women who died from the infectious diseases that swept like prairie fires through those schools. Although some of those children may have looked for their families to come and rescue them—there where immunity was low and where there was inadequate sanitation, poor nutrition, crowded conditions, and lonely despair— Death was usually the dark Horseman who came riding.

But it was not all negative. The Lakota medicine man Lame Deer would talk later in life about the songs and stories he learned from other students when they got together where no white teachers would hear them. By being brought together with Indians from many Native nations, Indian boarding school students learned a lot about other tribes. There were strictly enforced rules against contact between the male and female students—rules enforced by such punishments as locking recalcitrant students in basements or closets or beating those disobedient boys who waved at a girl across a room. ("If we had ever actually engaged in sex, they probably would have shot us," my Shawnee poet friend Barney Bush said.) Despite that, a lot of romances and marriages came out of boarding schools. In many cases, those marriages were as intertribal as the children of storyteller, musician, and hoop dancer Kevin Locke, a Lakota from North Dakota, and his wife, a Tlingit from southeast Alaska. They met at boarding school. A significant part of the new Indian identity is intertribal because of boarding school "matchmaking" that produced innumerable hyphenated offspring, kids who may have pairs of grandparents living a continent apart.

Many American Indian leaders of the late nineteenth century supported the idea of the boarding schools, knowing their children needed to know the ways of the white world for their people to survive. Spotted Tail, of the Brule Lakotas, was so convinced by Pratt's words that he sent five of his own children to that first class at Carlisle. Although many of those leaders would later regret their decisions to send their children to boarding schools, gradually Indian education began to change. Criticism of the boarding schools and the high cost of maintaining them led to the creation of day schools built on the reservations. Ironically, by the time the government closed down most of the boarding schools in the second half of the twentieth century, the institutions had become true Indian schools, controlled more by Native needs than government pipe dreams and offering courses of study that supported and encouraged traditions. The Haskell Institute, one of the few that still remains, is one such school. The Institute of American Indian Arts in Santa Fe, New Mexico, which was founded in 1962 to encourage a new generation of Native artists, is one of the best examples of what a true Indian education can be today. Young Native painters and potters, poets and sculptors are as eager to attend IAIA as some of their grandparents were to run away from the old Indian schools.

all is living around us: animal people and plants

IF WE DO NOT SHOW RESPECT

FOR THE BEAR WHEN WE KILL HIM,

HE WILL NOT RETURN.

—*traditional Mistassini Cree saying*

the bear helper

(CREE)

There was a man who had a Bear for a helper. In his dreams, that Bear spoke to him often, telling him where to find game animals. So, when he hunted, that man was always successful. But, after a while, that man stopped doing the things the Bear told him he had to do. He stopped showing respect for the animals he hunted and he wasted the meat.

Seeing this man's behavior, his helper grew displeased. One day, while the man was out hunting, the Bear came to his house and took away the man's son. He carried *the boy off with him to his den.*

When the man came home, he found his son gone. He saw the tracks of the Bear and knew what must have happened. He followed the tracks until they disappeared in the snow. All winter the boy was missing and the hunter grieved for him. He wept and wept, and finally the Bear took pity. He came to the man in a dream and spoke to him.

"If you want your son back, you must do as I say. Go into the forest and keep going toward the sunset until you cross a moose trail. Do not follow that moose, but continue on until you find a rabbit trail. Follow that rabbit's tracks through the snow and you will find your son."

As soon as the hunter woke, he went straight into the forest and went on until he saw the tracks of a moose in the snow. Those tracks led toward the north, but he crossed over them and continued on. At last he came to that rabbit trail, its tracks leading to the south. He followed those tracks until they came to a place where the snow was piled in a mound and it was yellow. He knew this was the Bear's den. He began to dig, calling out his son's name. From deep inside the den, his son answered him, "My Father, I am here."

Then the Bear came up out of his den, with the hunter's son right behind him. "Listen to me," the Bear said. "I am giving your son back to you. But you must do as I tell you. From now on you must always show respect to the animals you hunt. You must never waste their meat."

So it was that the hunter got back his son. From then on, he never forgot to show respect for the animals he hunted, and he never again wasted their meat.

The animals remember what humans forget. I have heard that said so many times by Native elders of so many different tribal nations, from Mohegan to Tlingit, that I cannot even begin to list them all. Though expressed in different

all is living around us: animal people and plants

words and in different languages, it always comes down to this—the Animal People are wiser than human beings because they do not forget to behave in the proper way. As my friend Jake Swamp, a Mohawk subchief, once put it to me, "The animals remember their original instructions from the Creator."

Seeing animals in human terms is called *anthropomorphism* in English. When I attended Cornell University it was to major in wildlife conservation. Though I know that many of my teachers (none of whom were American Indian) loved the natural world and its creatures, they always were careful to set themselves apart from and above it. As much as I respected them and enjoyed their classes, the time always came when, in any number of ways, they made it clear that it was romantic to imagine that animals could speak to one another, much less communicate with humans. To be fair to them, they had to do that. If they went one step further and imagined a sentient existence for plants, they were really going off the deep end. (It might be gently suggested that perhaps you had recently been earning a bit of extra money by taking part in those experiments the psychology department was doing with campus volunteers? The ones in which they give you those little pills?) The idea then was that nature was a great mechanism. Plants were like clocks, wound up by the seasons and ticking to the beat of impersonal chemical reactions. Animals were totally in the grip of instinct, born "knowing without knowing that they know."

During the three years I spent in wildlife conservation at Cornell, there were a lot of times when I bit my tongue. The only thing that helped was writing poems. In the world of poetry, being imaginative and illogical was okay. It helped me so much that I changed my major after my junior year and spent an extra year to get a degree in English. It was a decision that confused the hell out of the people who thought they knew me and even my wife-to-be, who thought she was marrying a naturalist who would take her off to live with him in the wilderness, wondering for a while what she had gotten into—although our last thirty-eight years together have found us never that far from truly wild places.

our stories remember

I think I know the exact day when something in me snapped, like the green branch of a tree twisted too hard by someone lost and pushing his way through the forest. It was during a lecture on wildlife management when the primary discussion focused on how shooting preserves could best be laid for duck hunters so that their feathered targets, when flushed from the ponds, would fly right over a perfectly designed hill that concealed the waiting humans and their twelve-gauge shotguns. Our job was to learn how to make hunting easy for men who were not even willing to exchange the sweat of a hard walk for the life of a single bird. Guaranteed game harvests. That was our business.

Later that same day, as I walked under a low autumn sky the scarred color of slate, I heard a sound overhead. Just above the clouds a flight of geese was passing. They were talking to one another. That was what my Abenaki grandfather always said the geese did—they talked to one another. Their yelping calls were so clear, so sharp, so insistently communicating—not just with one another but with everything that breathed and listened, from the ancient blue of Cayuga Lake to the deer in the field that also lifted its head—that they pierced my heart. I would have much preferred to fly off with those birds than go into that classroom again.

Seeing animals as of lesser value than humans has always been called foolishness in American Indian cultures. Not only traditional stories, but personal experience, taught the elders of all our nations that the Animal People care for their families, feel love and sympathy, anger and despair just as human beings do. By observing the animals, humans can learn many things. The way a mother bear cares for her cubs is a lesson for all human mothers. In fact, in one Native tradition after another, there are stories of how a bear may choose to also care for a human child. The Midwest Potawatomis tell about a little girl who becomes lost in the forest. No one is able to find her until several moons have passed and she is found, safe and well, sleeping in a den with a mother bear.

wolf songs of pity

The wolves also offer a lesson in child-rearing that I have heard cited again and again among different tribes. In a wolf pack, not only the parents, but the other adult animals, take part in feeding, watching over, and playing with the young. That is how it should be in a human village, where no child should ever be without caring adults.

I need to say more about the wolves because there are so many references to them in stories and so many places where their interactions with humans have been crucial to human growth and survival. At some time, long ago, a wolf came out of the forest and decided to remain with the people, to become the first dog. Stories of dogs and hunters, or dogs saving their masters, or even of dogs becoming people and marrying human beings are too numerous for me to even begin to list them. My novel *Dawn Land* has so much of its focus on the relationship between the main character, an Abenaki youth of long ago, and his dogs that some said it should have been named "Dog Land." Yet in its pages I only touched on the traditional knowledge and lore about dogs of one American Indian nation, my own Abenaki people. But those wolves that remained wolves have kept on talking to the people. The Lakota leader Sitting Bull was famous for composing songs, and at least one of his songs was given to him by a wolf. Not just the idea for the song, but its words, came from the wolf's mouth. The wolves taught us how to sing together. Those wolves, several of my Cheyenne friends have told me, like to talk to us. They tell us things, but not all of our people still remember how to understand them.

Sometimes, when the people were hungry and unable to find game, the wolves would take pity on the pitiful humans. They would come close to their camp and howl, telling those who could understand where they could find the buffalo herds. Among the Cheyenne who fled north from Oklahoma in that tragic autumn of 1878—when many Cheyennes who were being held captive in Fort Sill died while trying to escape back to their northern Montana homeland— was a wolf-talker named Pawnee Woman. The wife of Dull Knife, one of the Cheyenne chiefs, she understood the wolves. The night before she died, kicked by a horse while they tried to break camp quickly as soldiers approached, the wolves came close to the Cheyenne camp and howled. Several people remembered it well. They remembered Pawnee Woman telling them what the wolves said to her, warning them that the place they were headed toward was bad.

The idea of the Animal People having sympathy for us, taking pity on human beings, is as old and deep as the roots of the mountains. Why would they do so? Part of the reason for this may simply be because of a compassion for all beings as deep as that of the Buddha, who, in one of his incarnations, is said to have given up his physical life and offered his body as food for a starving tiger and her cubs. However, the line between human and animals is so lightly drawn in American Indian cultures that it ceases to exist at certain points. The ideas of totem and clan offer some clue to this connection. *Totem* is a word that comes from *ototeman,* an Anishinabe word roughly meaning "one's relative." There is a mystical connection between a human and his or her totem. That totem, which might be an animal, a plant, or a natural phenomenon, serves as the symbol of a tribe or a clan, a society. A totem is also seen by an individual as a guardian spirit. In general, if you have a certain creature as a totem, you would not hunt it.

Clan is a bond that goes beyond mere blood relations. Among the Iroquois, for example, your clan is always inherited from your mother, whether you are male or female. (It is only logical, a Mohawk friend said to me. After all, you always know who your mother is.) Those clans are usually identified by animals. Among the Five Iroquois Nations, for example, you always find the Bear, Turtle, and Wolf Clans. However, birds, aquatic creatures, plants, and even things that seem abstract to a Western mind may be clan identifiers. Thus the Cherokee clans include the Ball Clan and the Blue Clan.

all is living around us: animal people and plants

The being for which the clan is named is not, however, merely an abstraction or a symbol, but a reality at many levels. Going back to the Mohawks, I have been told (and have observed) that people who belong to a certain clan show certain characteristics that match those of their clan animal. Those who belong to the Turtle Clan, for example, may be more close-mouthed and reticent than those of the Wolf Clan. Clan is very important for American Indians. If an Iroquois man and woman belong to the same clan, they may not marry, even if they have no blood relationship and come from two different Iroquois nations located hundreds of miles apart. A similar taboo is found in the Southwest among the Diné. When two Navajo people meet for the first time, the proper thing to do is to introduce yourself by identifying first your mother's and then your father's clan. Even if you know nothing else about each other, a shared clan creates a bond of kinship and establishes certain rules of conduct. (In a certain school in New Mexico, the introduction of a class in ballroom dancing led to a great deal of tension between the teacher and some of her Navajo students who refused to take part. It turned out that she had tried to pair up boys and girls who were of the same clan. Dancing in that way with someone from your own clan would have been, in the traditional Navajo mind, the same as committing incest.)

The origin stories of certain totems and clans often have one element in common. Take, for example, the Penobscot story of the water monster who held back the waters of the river. When Gluskabe defeated that monster and the waters flowed again, many of the people were so thirsty that they jumped into the water and turned into such water creatures as fish, turtles, and frogs. Thus, certain Penobscot families have a sort of totem relationship to those particular animal beings. Origin stories among other Indian nations about the coming of the Bear Clan, the birth of the Eagle Clan, and so on all involve that transformation of a human ancestor into an animal or an animal into a human ancestor.

remembering our relatives

The pity of the Animal People for human beings comes from the many connections between us. Moreover, that pity not only meant offering physical help and spiritual and moral guidance for human behavior, but also included sacrifice. It is at this point that my discussion is going to make some people, especially those who are deeply opposed to all hunting, uncomfortable; but one of the deepest bonds between humans and animals is hunting. It is the simple truth that, in the natural world, one physical body often consumes another. If we believe that the physical body is all that there is, all that there ever will be, of a human, a fish, an animal, a bird—or a cabbage—then there is something awful about that hunger, that sacrifice of one physical body to feed another. My ancestors and those of every single American Indian on this planet hunted and killed for personal and community survival. In some places, American Indians and Inuit people still live this way. That is especially true in the northern part of the North American continent, where agriculture is, quite literally, impossible. Aside from the brief summer, when some regions of the Arctic offer a harvest of berries and some green plants, for three-quarters of the year survival depends on fishing and hunting.

If those same people can speak of animals as relatives, how can they kill them? Part of it is simply because they needed or still need to do so to survive. Modern people, who have others do their killing for them, may imagine that they have no blood on their hands. Some may even be able to allow themselves the luxury of living a vegetarian lifestyle and feeling rather virtuous about it. Yet, unless they live the life of total abnegation prescribed by the Jains of India (who may eat only fruits and walk naked, carrying a peacock feather they use to brush the ground before them so that they do not inadvertently trample on a single insect), they need to remember that their hands are far from clean, especially if they live in America. The American culture of consumption does more damage every day to the Earth's environment than entire American Indian nations did in ten thousand years. The simple act of building a new house or constructing a road wipes out or alters the habitat that was never damaged by the hunter who killed a deer in that now-vanished habitat.

Corny as that television commercial was in which a tear falls from the eye of Iron Eyes Cody as he observes a polluted stream, for centuries, American Indian people continued to mourn the loss of forests and plains, of game herds and great flocks of birds. My Mohawk friend Jake Swamp told me how his people still remember the passenger pigeons that fed his people. Passenger pigeons existed in migratory flocks of millions of birds until they were wiped out by white market hunters in the nineteenth century. "We Iroquois have this dance," Jake said, "for the passenger pigeons. As long as we do that dance, they will never be forgotten."

And in that dance, the spirits of the passenger pigeons still survive. The survival of the spirit. We are not just a physical body. The hunting traditions of American Indian nations and our old stories bear witness to that awareness. Among the Crees, tobacco is smoked before the moose is hunted. That tobacco is offered to the moose, and when a moose is killed, it is said to have accepted the pipe. But it does not end there. After it dies, that moose wakes up again in a new body. It realizes it has been treated respectfully and well and so will be willing to have its body sacrificed again in the future. But if a hunter did not do things properly, if that hunter killed wantonly and showed no gratitude or respect, failed to give thanks, then that hunter would be in grave danger. The Cherokees speak of Awi Usdi, Little Deer, who is the chief of the game animals. If any hunter behaves badly, Little Deer comes to him at night and cripples his hands with arthritis so that he cannot draw his bow.

the medicine voice

Not only the animals, but also the green things of this Earth, are seen as sacred and sentient. Among American Indians, imagining that the plants are unaware of us as we care for them and pick their fruit, as we cut their branches or uproot them from the earth, is called blindness. I've been told many times by American Indian women and men who have learned the secrets of healing through medicine plants, that they were told by the plants themselves how to use them. That knowledge came to them in a dream or they heard it spoken by a breathless voice while they walked or sat in the forest.

As with hunting or fishing, there is a proper way to harvest plants. For example, one should never pick the first medicine plant you see, but make certain there are plenty of others. Even then, you do not pick too many or take the largest one. Before you gather any plant, you must speak to it, ask its permission, and offer a gift—such as some tobacco or beads. Then, when you reach for that plant, it will seem to leap into your hand. But if your mind is in the wrong place, if you are angry or confused or in a hurry, the medicine plants will hide from you. You cannot hear the medicine voice.

An Abenaki friend of mine went to get sweetgrass from a spot near the road where her late father had planted it years ago. She was in a hurry to get there and get back. She parked her car, got out, and wandered around for an hour trying to find the sweetgrass. Finally, sadly, she concluded that someone had pulled it all up or it had been killed by the road crews spreading salt. But when she told her mother about it, her mother's response was "Get the car." The two of them went back, and my friend parked right where she had been before. Her mother got out first. "Look here," her mother said. There was the sweetgrass, growing right next to the car.

between the worlds

A few years ago I stood on the southeastern edge of Glacier National Park. A trail in front of me led into the Two Medicine area to end at a lake surrounded by mountains that seemed to have been carved out of clouds and sky turned into stone. Just past the ranger station that marks the park boundary, a new sign indicated the trail to Running Eagle Falls. The small river fed by Two Medicine Lake winds next to the footpath, where an abundance of such food plants as flowering raspberry draw the attention of black bears and grizzlies, like the one whose fresh, berry-studded scat lay ahead of me just to the side of the trail—a reminder that this is still a place where the wild intersects with human lives. Sometimes that intersection leads to tragic results for both bear and human. People have been killed by bears in Glacier Park, and the local newspaper that morning told of the "humane destruction" of yet another "problem grizzly" that had kept returning from his forced relocations to raid the easy pickings of campsites.

Then, as the small forest opened up before me, I saw the falls, and my breath was drawn from me by its power. For Running Eagle Falls comes throbbing through the center of a wall of granite, pulsing out of a throat of stone below the steep cliffs, the sweet lifeblood of the land flowing forth. I could understand why this has always been a place for the Blackfeet people to seek a vision, and the story of Running Eagle came alive for me.

Here, Blackfeet elders say, the woman known as Running Eagle came to climb the cliff above the falls and seek a vision. It was not something that Blackfeet women did then, but she felt a great need to leap over that threshold, to gain the power a vision would grant her. Her husband had been killed by enemies. When, after waiting alone in that cold and dangerous place, waiting without food or drink for four nights and days, that vision did come to her, it gave her the strength to help her people. She returned to lead them as a war chief, to help them for many years as a leader. When she died, the burial scaffold that held her body was placed in the trees on the steep mountainside above that waterfall.

Such thresholds of power are found everywhere in this land, spots known by Native people to be crossing-over places. It is there that the spirits of the land, the animal powers that choose at times to speak to humans, make themselves heard and seen. Some of those places are as spectacularly beautiful as Running Eagle Falls, and many of them are to be found in those mountainous places where the land rises up to brush the clouds, where—as my Abenaki ancestors put it in their translation of the Lord's Prayer—*dali kik ali kik togwadets,* "here on Earth it is the same as in the Sky Land." In such a place you may feel yourself to be at the center of all things, as Black Elk felt when he stood on top of Harney Peak and had his great vision recorded by John Neihardt in *Black Elk Speaks.*

There is also a danger to be found in those places—or perhaps to be found in us when we come close to the hub of things, to the intersection where we can cross over, however briefly, and become empowered. Our traditional stories are often cautionary tales and guides to behavior when we come to those doorways. When we pass through, we may be totally changed, we may even create a whole new world, or—if our minds are not straight and we are confused—we may bring confusion and even death to others and to ourselves. Leaping over the threshold is not something to be undertaken lightly.

As I walked that path to Running Eagle Falls in Glacier National Park, following a trail first made by the feet of the great bears, one such story was in my mind. It is one told throughout the range of the grizzly, the tale of the Girl Who Married a Bear. One of the most memorable is from Southeast Alaska and told by Tlingit storyteller Nora Marks Dauenhauer in *Haa Shuka.* David Rockwell, in his book *Giving Voice to Bear,* provides one of the best discussions I've yet read of this widespread tradition, focusing on one particular telling from Maria Johns, a Tagish woman of the lower Yukon. So many versions have been collected of this story that even a simple listing of them would take many pages.

all is living around us: animal people and plants

Like so many of our Native teaching traditions, every version I've heard of this story begins with human error. A young woman is out gathering berries with her family or with other girls of her own age. She finds a pile of bear droppings in the middle of the path. She has been cautioned not to jump over bear droppings. But she disregards the advice she has been given. She speaks insulting words about the bear who has passed there. Then she leaps over the bear droppings. In so doing, she has crossed over the threshold. She has drawn the attention of the bear and entered into his world. Soon after this, she falls behind the others and is approached by someone she thinks to be a handsome young man. He is a bear, however, and he carries her off to his cave to be his wife.

Sometimes, it seems, there are certain thresholds that we humans should not cross. Only a deep awareness of the consequences of our actions can guide us toward the right decision. The same day that Montana newspaper carried the account of the destruction of a "problem" bear, there was a long article about a Blackfeet man's plea that the killing of grizzlies as a control measure be ended. He asked that the authorities respect the bears, that even when killing is the only alternative, certain measures common to all our Algonquin nations when we take the life of a bear should be followed. Prayers should be spoken, and there are proper ways to treat the bear's body. Even better, he suggested, instead of killing the bears, give them to the Blackfeet Nation and allow the Blackfeet to set up a special place on their large reservation around Glacier National Park to keep those bears in safety.

Then the man related a story. When he was a young child, he was out walking with his grandmother and they encountered a giant grizzly coming toward them on the path. They did not run away or try to confront the bear. Instead, his grandmother placed her blanket over her own head and the head of her small grandson as they stood there beside the path. The bear then calmly walked past them, its great paws leaving tracks in the earth, its passage marking a way of mutual respect.

Recommended Reading

Hogan, Linda (Chickasaw). *Dwellings.* New York: Norton, 1996. These essays on the natural world and its creatures come from one of Native America's finest poets.

Marshall, Joseph, III (Sicangu Lakota). *On Behalf of the Wolf and the Native People.* Santa Fe: Red Crane Books, 1995. Marshall's essays on contemporary American Indian life range from his reflections on his experiences as an extra during the making of *Dances with Wolves* to a thoughtful consideration of the relationship between wolves and Indians.

Matthews, John Joseph (Osage). *Talking to the Moon: Wildlife Adventures on the Plains and Prairies of Osage Country.* Norman: University of Oklahoma Press, 1945. This wonderful autobiography is equally influenced by the work of Thoreau and Muir and the traditions of the author's Osage people.

tobacco

*A great blessing will come
to the people of the Longhouse.
This Tobacco is a great gift to the people.*

—*Mohawk tradition*

There is a story told by the Ho-Chunk people of the upper Midwest about tobacco. Soon after the world was made, the Great Spirit called all the beings together.

"I have one more thing to give to the world," the Great Spirit said. "It is a powerful thing called tobacco. I will always listen to whoever burns tobacco and prays. To whom shall I give this tobacco?"

The various beings then debated about who would get this powerful gift. The winds thought they should receive it. The waters and the stones each said that it should be theirs. Every invisible spirit, every bird, every animal, everything that flew or burrowed in the earth or crawled, even every other plant wanted the tobacco. Everything that had power said that their power entitled them to the tobacco—that they were so strong, the tobacco should be theirs.

The Great Spirit listened and then decided.

"I will give the tobacco to human beings. I will not give it to them because they are strong, but because they are weak. They are the weakest and most confused things in Creation, and so they are in need of tobacco, for it will make their prayers stronger. When they use tobacco in the right way, when they burn it and pray, everything in Creation will listen to them, and I will always pay heed to their prayers."

And so it is to this day.

The list of useful plants that were domesticated by American Indian agronomists is staggering. More than 150 species, many of which are now crucial to the world economy, were first grown by American Indian farmers. These include varieties of beans, squash, and corn, potatoes, sweet potatoes, peppers, tomatoes, avocados, chiles, so-called Egyptian cotton, peanuts, vanilla, and the cocoa from which chocolate was first made by the Native peoples of Mexico. If you removed every item in a supermarket that had some part of its origin in American Indian agriculture, most of the shelves would be bare. The two plants that have been of the greatest commercial value, however, include one that is universally praised and one that is truly the most controversial legally grown plant in the world. The former is corn; the latter, of course, is tobacco.

It seems that tobacco was well known to and used by the majority of American Indian tribal nations throughout the Americas. Invariably, rather than using it purely for pleasure, tobacco was associated with ritual and prayer. Among many of the Native nations of North America, the ceremonial smoking of a pipe together made one's breath visible and was the equivalent to the modern practice of swearing an oath on a Bible to prove that one is speaking the truth. Tobacco would be burned in a fire to carry one's prayers in its smoke up to the Creator. It would be placed on the ground to give thanks when one gathered medicine plants. In many Native nations, tobacco was sometimes smoked in a more or less non-sacramental manner in a personal pipe. However, those who smoked that way were the old people, for tobacco is said to have been given as a comfort to the old.

When Sir Walter Raleigh first introduced tobacco to England in the early seventeenth century, its use became as controversial then as the use of cocaine is now. (Coca, from which cocaine is derived, is another Native plant that was turned from a useful part of everyday life into an addictive drug. In the Andes, chewing coca leaves makes it possible to work at high altitudes. Virtually everyone carries a bag of coca leaves around their necks to use in this way. The result of chewing coca leaves is not a drug high. It counteracts the exhaustion, nausea, and headaches one may experience at those altitudes and creates a mild feeling of euphoria.) Smoking tobacco—called "sotweed"—was at first reviled in England as a filthy and addictive habit. Many prominent figures tried to make it an illegal substance. However, it soon became a lucrative export crop of the Virginia Colony and the most profitable commercial plant per acre. The huge commercial success of tobacco made cigarette manufacturers among the wealthiest of Americans by the mid-twentieth century. Despite the fact that the regular smoking of tobacco has been identified as a major cause of cancer and other illnesses, the tobacco lobby remains one of the most successful and politically powerful forces in American industry and politics.

American Indians as a whole still use and revere tobacco as a sacred plant. Most American Indians carry it with them when they travel. I have often heard it said by Native elders that it is not the use of tobacco, but its misuse for selfish reasons, that has made it such a threat to human health.

epilogue:
the drum is the heartbeat

THE ENTIRE CREATION STILL FOLLOWS THOSE INSTRUCTIONS OF

LIFE. THE TREES, THE FRUITS, THEY NEVER FAIL.... WE SEE THE

CREATION...LIFE, THE CIRCLE, A MEASUREMENT WITH NO

BEGINNING AND NO ENDING.

   —*Phillip Deere (Muskogee/Creek), from a speech given to*

   a U.N. Conference in Geneva, Switzerland, September 1977

the seventh direction

(LAKOTA)

In the beginning, Wakan Tanka, the Great Mystery, made all things. Then Wakan Tanka took the four directions and put them where they should be in the Place of the Sunrise, the Place of Summer, the Place of the Sunset, and the Place of Winter. Then Wakan Tanka put the Sky above and the Earth below.

So the six directions were now all in their right places. And now Wakan Tanka held only one final direction, a Seventh Direction. This Seventh Direction was the most powerful of all, for it contained the true knowledge of the spirit. If anyone could find this direction, they, too, would gain great power. This troubled Wakan Tanka, for he knew that the human beings who were soon to come would want this power. If it was too easy to find, they would take it for granted and use it foolishly. So Wakan Tanka decided to hide the Seventh Direction in a place that would be hard for human beings to look.

Because the Animal People are wise beings, Wakan Tanka called them to a council to suggest where the Seventh Direction might be hidden. Because the humans would have no wings, Eagle suggested hiding it above the sky. But that would not do, for Wakan Tanka knew that humans were clever and would find a way to fly above the sky. Bear wanted to place it deep inside a cave under a mountain, but Wakan Tanka knew that the humans would dig deep below the deepest caves if they suspected something of value was there. Fish thought the dark bottom of the sea would work, but Wakan Tanka knew that humans would bring light even to the deepest part of the ocean.

At last, Mole whispered his idea to Wakan Tanka and Wakan Tanka agreed. There, just as Mole suggested, the Seventh Direction was placed. Where was that hidden spot? It was in every person's heart. That is the best hiding place of all, for one of the hardest things a human can do is to look into his or her heart. If you have the honesty and courage to truly look into your heart, you will be ready to find the Seventh Direction.

the place of the heart

CaNte Ista. "Through the eye of the heart." Those are the words in Lakota used to describe a way of seeing that is good and true. When one has crawled out of the *inipi,* the sweat lodge, that small, dome-shaped structure used by many of our peoples for self-purification and prayer, through the heart is the way one sees. Within that small lodge, the red-hot stones have throbbed with heat, as alive and vibrant as a heartbeat. The scent of sweetgrass and cedar have filled one's senses. The steam has risen as water was poured on the stones. Strong old songs of healing and thanks have risen as well. Cleansed of the impurities of spirit and body by using the four great powers of the world—earth, air, fire, and water—one may now perceive things in a different way.

CaNte Ista. Through the eye of the heart. The breath of the wind touches you and you see how everything is a circle, everything is part of the cycles of life and breath, everything continues.

The spiritual and symbolic place of the heart is just as central to the many different American Indian cultures as the physical heart is within the body of a human being. When the heart is in the right place, when a person is in true alignment with everything that is touched by the heartbeat, then there is true balance and peace. All things are equal and related to one another. It is a very democratic thing, that vision of the heart. I have heard it said, in fact, that the heart of a good chief beats with the heart of the people. The heart of a chief is in the center of the circle of the nation. So the good chief is like the heart in that he works for everyone, not just for himself.

The heart is literally the center and source of life. It is like the fire in the lodge that enables the people to survive the winter. When that fire goes out we perish. The heart, California Indian people say, is fire. Without a heart, life cannot continue. One of the oldest understandings among hunters is that a wound to the

epilogue: the drum is the heartbeat

heart is invariably fatal. Hunting has been of vital importance to every American Indian culture. A good hunter knew the place of an animal's heart and how to aim an arrow or spear to strike that mortal spot. A common motif in American Indian art, especially among the people of the Great Plains, is an x-ray drawing of an animal with a line extending from its mouth to its heart. When the line of breath to the heart is cut, life ends. That is the natural way of things.

On the other hand, when the heart is unnatural (the Diné say that when someone becomes a "skin-walker," taking on the shape of an animal to do evil, that person has not one but two hearts) or removed by sorcery from its normal location, then the balance is broken. When the heart is wrong, behavior that is dangerous and antisocial to the point of chaos and evil enters the world.

We see this in a Cattaraugus Seneca tale, "Turkey Boy Squeezed the Hearts of Sorcerers." Related by George Jimerson in 1903 and published twenty years later by Arthur C. Parker in his landmark volume *Seneca Myths and Folk Tales,* it is a story filled with symbolic and direct references to the heart. A boy named Turkey lives with his grandmother in a "lonely lodge a long ways from a settlement." One day, she shows him a hidden room full of clothing and weapons and many strange things, among them a great drum. She tells him these things belonged to his family. Now, however, all the other people are gone. They have been devoured by a monster wizard who eats human flesh. His lodge is to the east in the midst of a bed of strawberries as large as human hearts. (The relationship of the shape of the strawberry to the heart is an interesting one that we see in other Native American traditions. In the Cherokee story of First Man and First Woman, First Woman leaves her husband because they quarrel. Grandmother Sun, the Great Apportioner, stops her by making the first strawberries, each shaped like a human heart, grow in her path. They are so sweet to the taste that First Woman stops to pick some for her husband, allowing him to catch up to her and beg her pardon. So it is that the sharing of strawberries is associated with the love and understanding found in our hearts.)

Turkey is fascinated by the story his grandmother has told. The next day, while she is away, he returns to the hidden room. He finds a lacrosse stick and a ball and plays with it. Then he begins to beat the drum. He beats it so loudly that his grandmother returns, fearful that the sound will lead the monster wizard to them. "Tell me more about the monster," he demands. Finally his grandmother reveals that the cannibal wizard is named Deadoendjadasen and that he has seven sisters. "Make me a pair of moccasins," Turkey says. Then, wearing those moccasins made by his grandmother, Turkey sets out toward the east.

Upon reaching the monster's lodge, which is indeed surrounded by those strawberries as large as hearts, Turkey sees a strange thing. A human skin tied to a cord is hung from a pole to keep watch on the lodge while Deadoendjadasen is away. To avoid being seen, Turkey shrinks down to the size of a mole and burrows over to the pole. He persuades the Skin Boy to tell him more about the monster, promising to set Skin Boy free after he destroys the monster. Skin Boy then tells him that the wizard and his seven sisters have all removed their hearts from their bodies so that they cannot be killed. (This is a common motif in American Indian traditions. Another notable example of it can be found in Chippewa Cree storyteller Ron Evans's wonderful telling of the story of "Round Like a Ball Boy," in which the hero discovers that the hearts of the cannibal monsters are hung in a tree.) The eight hearts are hidden under the wing of a loon that swims in a little pool beneath the bed in Deadoendjadasen's lodge. Turkey obtains the hearts and, when the seven evil sisters and Deadoendjadasen try to catch him, he weakens them by squeezing their hearts and finally kills them by hurling their hearts, one by one, onto a rock, where they "each cracked open like a flint stone." He then frees Skin Boy—who becomes fully alive and human at his touch and turns out to be his lost brother—and brings back to life all of his people the cannibal wizard has eaten.

Just as has been the case in many other cultures around the world, for most Native Americans the heart has been and remains associated with aspects of emotion and cognition that modern science now attributes solely to the brain. Rather than seeing this as a lack of sophistication on the part of Native people, it might be remembered that despite all evidence to the contrary, the heart still holds its place as the symbol of love for the Western world. And a heart made of stone is not just found in American Indian stories.

Moreover, there is a great deal of logic to the symbolism of the heart found in American Indian cultures. The first lesson that we learn, Mohegan people say, is from the heart. Harold Tantaquidgeon, a Mohegan elder, explained that to me many years ago while he was cutting wood outside the Mohegan Indian Museum in Uncasville, Connecticut. A child's first job is to listen, he said, his words punctuated by the rhythmic thud of the ax into the maple log. That was as far as he went with words. As with many things I've been taught by elders, the full meaning of that didn't hit me until many years later as I thought back on that day and realized that the thumping regularity of each ax strike was much the same as the beat of a drum...or a heart.

The heartbeat is the first sound a child hears. Before that child draws breath, tastes food with her mouth, or places her feet upon the earth, the child hears the heartbeat of her mother. In those many months before birth, the baby moves with the rhythm of the mother's heart and dances to that first song. Then, when a child has entered this world, seen the light, breathed the air, begun to walk, that child's feet are ready to dance when she hears the beating of a drum.

The place of the heart is also the place of the drum. Remember that drum found by Turkey in the hidden room. The heart and the drum are inextricably connected. It is there in our languages. In Abenaki, the word for heart is *pahko*. To create the word for drum, we add the suffix ligan, which roughly means "to make something." *Pahkoligan,* the Abenaki word for the drum, might then be translated as "that which makes a drum." This Native American connection between the drum and the heart is universal, though not every Native language makes it quite so explicit. The mother's heart, the drum, and all of life itself are connected by the common understanding—frequently voiced at powwows around the continent, where the ceremonial fire and the drum are at the center of everything—that "the Drum is the heartbeat of Mother Earth."

That is where the true place of the heart is—within that circle where all things are connected. The heart is the metronome keeping the rhythm that is all of life. If we ever forget our place in the great circle, all we have to remember is to listen to our hearts. There we will find again that music given us by our birth. In the heart is the source of every song. It is the place where all our stories begin and begin again.

deer

Down from the places of magic,
down from the places of magic,
the winds blow and from my antlers
and from my ears they gather stronger...

—*Pima Deer Song*

There is a story told by the Cree people about a hunter who went to live with the deer. He had become lost, and when he stumbled into the village of the Deer People he thought at first they were human beings. He fell in love with a Deer woman and they married. Then she told him who her people were and that it was all right for him to hunt the deer. As long as he hunted in the proper way, never taking more than he needed, never wasting the meat, always showing respect for the bones, then each deer that he killed would come back to life again in the Deer Village. The Deer People would survive and so would the human beings. He stayed with them so long that his wife had a little girl. The hunter loved his wife and daughter, but he became lonely for his own people. Seeing how he felt, his wife urged him to return to his own village. But she asked him to promise her two things. "Promise me that you will never forget that I am your wife. Promise me also that you will never kill a white deer."

The hunter agreed, but as soon as he was among his own people, he forgot his promises. He married again, and as soon as he did so, a white deer began to appear on a hill at the edge of the forest each evening, looking down at the village. His new human wife saw the white deer.

"Kill that deer for me," she said to the hunter. "I want its hide."

The man did as his second wife asked. But as soon as his arrow struck the white deer, it turned into his daughter. His Deer wife stepped from the forest, picked up the body of their child, and then disappeared—never to be seen again. Although that hunter looked long and hard, he was never able to find the village of the Deer People again. But he passed on what the Deer taught him to the other humans. So it is to this day that no one will kill a white deer, and as long as every hunter always remembers to show the proper respect, the deer will always sacrifice their bodies to help the people.

The deer played the same role for the people of the eastern woodlands that the buffalo played for the Plains nations. The deer was the primary source of both meat and skins to be used as clothing. Story after story makes it clear that the destinies of deer and humans are deeply intertwined and that the deer we hunt will allow themselves to be taken as long as we behave properly as hunters. (The importance of being a good hunter among American Indians can be seen by looking at our traditional tales. In nation after nation, all across the continent, the hero of the story is often a good hunter whose adventures occur while he is out seeking game for his people.)

Deer songs, which praise the deer, are frequently found among the nations of the Southwest, where Deer is a deeply sacred animal to such peoples as the Diné, the Hopis, the Pueblo Nations, and the O'odhams. In Tucson, Arizona, people are allowed each year to witness the beautiful Deer Dance, which connects the Yaqui people to the magical Flower World, a place of healing and magic presided over by the Deer. My friend Harold Littlebird, who is Santo Domingo/Laguna, has written a whole suite of contemporary poems in English about the Deer. He told me how his people will sometimes put corn pollen and little pieces of turquoise in the tracks of the deer as they follow them, offerings to the spirits of those creatures they hope to use for their food.

Sources and other versions of the stories

In all cases, the traditional stories in this volume are my own tellings, but they are not original. I have drawn on both the written versions cited and oral tellings shared with me in the past. As always, the stories know more than I do, and any mistakes in them are my own. Here are a list of acknowledgments and further information about these tales.

the road of stories

"The Journey" (Arapaho): Various tellings of this story are found among a number of the nations of the northern Plains. A discussion of the Omaha version of this story can be found in *The World's Rim: Great Mysteries of the American Indian,* by Hartley Burr Alexander (Cambridge, Mass.: University Press, 1916). The Arapaho version is described in *The People of the Center: American Indian Religion and Christianity,* by Carl Starkloff (New York: The Seabury Press, 1974).

who are we?

"Great Hare Makes the People" (Powhatan): This is one of the first American Indian stories recorded by an Englishman. In 1610, around Christmas, Captain Samuel Argall invited Iopassus, a Powhatan elder, on board his ship after trading with him. As they sat by the hearth, one of the Englishmen was reading a Bible. After noticing that Iopassus seemed interested in what was being read, Argall asked Henry Spellman, an English boy who had lived as a guest among the Indians for a year, to translate the story of Genesis, which Iopassus "seemed to like well of. Howbeit he bade the captain, if he would hear, he would tell him the manner of *their* beginning, which was a pretty fabulous tale indeed," according to *The History of Travel into Virginia Brittania: The First Book of the First Decade,* by William Strachey. (Completed in 1612, but not published until 1758, Strachey's work was preserved in three manuscripts in the Bodleian Library. In this case I have quoted from the volume *Jamestown Narratives: Eyewitness Account of the Virginia Colony,* edited and with commentary by Edward Wright Haile, Champlain, Va.: Roundhouse, 1998.)

origins

"The Great Rock" (Omaha): Francis La Flesche, the Omaha writer who is also the author of *The Middle Five, The Omaha, and Ke-Ma-Ha: 100 Osage Stories,* recorded a version of this story that was published in the *27th Annual Report of the Bureau of American Ethnology* in 1911. I have also retold the Lakota version of this story that appears in *Keepers of the Earth* (Golden, Colo.: Fulcrum Publishing, 1999).

"How the Earth Was Made" (Seneca): There may have been more versions of this story told in print than any other American Indian tale. Few Native nations have had more written about them than the Six Nations of the Iroquois (as the original five Nations became known when the Tuscaroras from North Carolina joined them in the eighteenth century), and almost every book on the Iroquois either mentions or retells this story. It is also a very popular theme for the new generation of Six Nations artists, and there are innumerable Indian-made images of this story drawn, painted, carved in stone, bone, and wood, shaped in clay, even presented in film and video. One of the best published sources for this story is Arthur C. Parker's *Seneca Myths and Folk Tales,* first published in 1923 by the Buffalo Historical Society and reissued by the University of Nebraska in 1989. As far as those who have told me this story or discussed it with me, there are too many for me to mention them all. However, I have to offer special thanks to Ray Tehanetorens Fadden and his son, John Kahionhes Fadden, whose words and images have helped me for many years as I have tried to gain a deeper understanding of this story and other Mohawk traditions.

"The Emergence of the People" (Diné): This is one of the most frequently published (and frequently mistold) stories in all of American Indian tradition literature. Virtually every book written about the Navajos includes a version. I could not have done this retelling, which corrects some of the most commonly made errors, without the invaluable assistance of Harry Walters (Diné) who teaches courses in traditional culture at Diné College in Tsaile, Arizona, and has carefully reviewed everything I have written about Diné culture over the last few years.

spirit: life and death

"The Coming of Death" (Western Shoshone): The story of how death came to the people as a result of a choice made by Old Man, Coyote, or some other ancient being is so common among the Native peoples of the West and Northwest that I have heard at least a dozen different tellings of this story and I know of at least that many written versions. In Anne M. Smith's *Shoshone Tales* (Salt Lake City: University of Utah Press, 1993), "Controversy Over Death" is the first story in the book. The book owes a great deal to two remarkable Western Shoshone women, the late Anna Premo and her daughter, Beverly Crum. The addition of the nonsense sound *pai* at the end of Coyote's sentences and certain other vocal mannerisms in both Coyote's and Wolf's speech reflect the way the stories are told in Shoshone. Unique speech patterns and ways of pronouncing words are common Native storytelling devices. In many of our languages, for example, whenever a Trickster speaks, he or she has a very nasal voice.

trickster's turn

"Iktomi and the Ducks" (Lakota): I have heard versions of this story told from the East Coast through the Great Plains. In the Northeast, the Trickster is Manabozho; among the Cheyenne it is Wihio or Veho. In the eastern woodlands and Great Lakes regions, the birds tricked are ducks. In the West, the prairie chickens are duped through the trickster's foul play. Paul Radin's *The Trickster* (New York: Dell Publishing Co., 1956) contains what is probably the best-known version of this story. However, this story is still very much alive among Native people. When the Lakota storyteller Kevin Locke shared it with me a decade ago, he pointed out that he not only knew the story, but also the song that Iktomi sang while the ducks danced with their eyes closed.

"Trickster's Black Shirt" (Ho-Chunk): I have heard this widely told story from a number of people over the years. As in the case of "Iktomi and the Ducks," Radin's *The Trickster* contains the best-known version.

"Trickster's Hands" is another widely told tale with many versions in print, including one in Radin's *The Trickster.*

"The Car That Hummed Along" and other Laughing Louis stories have been shared with me by such Maine Indian tradition-bearers as Wayne Newell (Passamaquoddy). Several Laughing Louis stories are collected in *The Wabanakis of Maine and the Maritimes* (Bath, Maine: American Friends Service Committee, 1989).

"The Telephone Pole Sweat" (Cheyenne): As I indicate in the text, this story was told to me by Lance Henson. It is his story.

"The Camp of Foolish People" (Chiricahua Apache): This tale and seven other stories of the Foolish People can be found in Morris Opler's *Myths and Tales of the Chiricahua Apache,* published in 1942 by the American Folklore Society.

Sources and other versions of the stories

"Exactly Five Pounds" (Western Abenaki): Speck's "Penobscot Tales and Religious Beliefs" (*Journal of American Folklore*, Jan.–March 1935) includes a version of this story called "The Trader Whose Hand Weighed a Pound" and indicates the story took place on the Saco River. Our own Western Abenaki traditions say that it was the Connecticut.

"The Older Brother" (Plains Cree): Verne Dusenberry's *The Montana Cree: A Study in Religious Persistence* (Norman: University of Oklahoma Press, 1998; orig. pub. in 1963) contains a version of this story. I have also heard other stories in which two or three of the Tricksters sit down and engage in such a contest. There is even an unpublished play on this subject written by the young Laguna Pueblo playwright Lee Francis IV.

contact: the coming of europeans

"A Friend of the Indians" (Seneca): One version of this can be found in Arthur C. Parker's biography *Red Jacket: Seneca Chief* (Lincoln: University of Nebraska Press, 1998). Similar stories told about other American Indians—including a story in which the Indian is talking with Abraham Lincoln—are found in a number of eastern and midwestern tribes.

"The Coming of the White People" (Paiute): Jarold Ramsey's wonderful compilation of traditional tales from Oregon, *Coyote Was Going There* (Seattle: University of Washington Press, 1977), contains a version of this entitled "White Men Are Snakes." Spoken by Piudy, a Paiute, it was originally recorded by Isabel Kelly in "Northern Paiute Tales," *Journal of American Folklore,* vol. 51, 1938.

"A Lover of Horses" (Nez Perce): As I mention in the text, my friend Phil George related this personal story to me.

"Name Allotment" (Creek): As I note in the text, this is a personal story of Louis Littlecoon Oliver's. He is the only source and gave me his permission to relate it.

generations: parents, grandparents, children

"Gluskonba's Grandmother" (Abenaki): The stories of the powerful but foolish Gluskonba (or Gluskabe or Glooskap) are widely told among the Abenaki people. Other versions of this story can be found in Frank Speck's "Penobscot Tales and Religious Beliefs" in the Jan.–March 1935 issue of the *Journal of American Folklore,* in Charles Godfrey Leland's *Algonquin Legends* (New York: Houghton Mifflin, 1884), and in many other places. I have also heard parts of this story from many people, including the late, deeply talented Abenaki artist Guy Sioui. One interesting recent spin on the story is that Gluskonba, while an ancient being, may also represent the powerful but uninformed white man, while Grandmother Woodchuck is the embodiment of Native wisdom. My sister Margaret has been looking into this as a result of her research into certain Micmac stories and the English traditional story of a voyage to Newfoundland made a century before Columbus by Lord Sinclair.

"Half a Blanket" (Mohawk): I have been told that there is also a story much like this told in Ireland. Whether its origin is European or American, it certainly connects to a number of other traditional Native stories in which a person is either abandoned or about to be abandoned and the foolishness of such a decision is then made clear by the end of the story. One version of this story, recorded in the Mohawk language, can be found in the New York State Museum Bulletin *Mohawk Tales.*

all is living around us: animal people and plants

"The Bear Helper" (Cree): The story of a bear abducting (or adopting) a human child and then taking that child to its den to sleep away the winter is a very widespread one. In virtually every case, a lesson is taught to adults as a result of the bear's actions. The Iroquois story of "The Boy Who Lived with the Bears," for example, teaches adults that it is their responsibility to care for all children as lovingly as does a mother bear. I have heard similar tales among the Abenakis of the Northeast and the Pueblos of the Southwest (my friend and teacher Swift Eagle told me the Santo Domingo Pueblo story of the Bear Boy thirty years ago). Bear serving as a spirit guide for hunters is a common theme in the northern part of the continent. In fact, Bear may even tell a hunter how to hunt that very bear itself. If it is treated properly after being killed—for example, its skull is placed in a tree—it will come back to life again. In a Seneca story related by Arthur C. Parker in *Seneca Myths and Folk Tales,* when Bear is shot by an arrow and "killed," it throws down a bag full of meat and keeps on running. Its body may perish, but its spirit is immortal. Robert Brightman's *Acaoohkiwina and Acimowina: Traditional Narratives of the Rock Cree Indians* (Quebec: Canadian Museum of Civilization, 1989) contains a version of this story told by Johny Bighetty.

epilogue: the drum is the heartbeat

"The Seventh Direction" (Lakota): This is *an apapa,* or "just so" story, that I learned from Lakota flute player and tradition keeper Kevin Locke. The concept of the heart being the Seventh Direction is a common one to many of our Native traditions, but I know of no story that illustrates it as well as this one Kevin shared with me. Kevin has recorded many albums of his music and stories, and he has recorded his version of this tale more than once, including on his audiotape *The Seventh Direction.*

sources for epigraphs

introduction: connections Fidelia Fielding/Flying Bird (Mohegan), 1925, from "Mu'ndu Wi'go: Mohegan Poems," by Joseph Bruchac, *Blue Cloud Quarterly,* 1978, translated from "A Mohegan Pequot Diary," *Bureau of American Ethnology Bulletin* 43 (1925).

the road of stories Anonymous Winnebago speaker, circa 1923, from "The Winnebago Tribe," by Paul Radin, *Bureau of American Ethnology Bulletin* 37 (1923).

who are we? Sandoval, Hastin Tlo'tsi Hee/Old Man Buffalo Grass (Navajo), 1928, from "The Diné: Origin Myths of the Navajo Indians," by Aileen O'Bryan, *Bureau of American Ethnology Bulletin* 163 (1956).

origins Chief Joseph (Nez Perce), 1879, from "An Indian's View of Indian Affairs," by Chief Joseph, *North American Review* 127 (April 1879).

spirit: life and death Ancient Passamaquoddy song, translated circa 1897 by J. D. Prince and published in *The Wabanakis of Maine and the Maritimes* (Bath, Maine: American Friends Service Committee, 1989).

trickster's turn Chapter Five: Yellowman (Diné), 1969, from "The Pretty Language of Yellowman," by Barre Tolkein, Genre 2 (1969).

contact: the coming of europeans Wahunsunacock (Powhatan), 1609, from *The Complete Works of John Smith,* vol. 1, edited by Philip L. Barbour (Chapel Hill: University of North Carolina Press, 1986).

generations: parents, grandparents, children Luther Standing Bear (Lakota), 1931, from *My Indian Boyhood,* by Luther Standing Bear (Lincoln: University of Nebraska Press, 1931).

all is living around us: animal people and plants Traditional Mistassini Cree saying, shared with Joseph Bruchac by a Cree elder.

epilogue: the drum is the heartbeat Phillip Deere (Muskogee/Creek), 1977, from a speech to a United Nations Conference in Geneva, Switzerland, and published in *Akwesasne Notes,* December 1977.

index

index